BLANKET THE TOWN

A knitted blanket that meets you where you live.

Margaret Holzmann

Integrity Ink

Oxnard, California

published by Integrity Ink

3749 Ocean Drive

Oxnard, CA 93035

www.theknitwit.org

Copyright © 2025 by Margaret Holzmann

Illustrations by Margaret Holzmann

Photography by Margaret Holzmann

ISBN 979-8-9855612-2-7

BLANKET THE TOWN KNITTING PATTERN

SIZE 54.5 x 71.5"/138 x 182 cm

TECHNIQUES Pu&k, short rows, 3-needle BO, sewing, embroidery, fair isle and intarsia color work.

YARN Rowan Yarns, Felted Tweed, DK (50% wool; 25% alpaca; 25% viscose; 191 yds/175 m; 1.75 oz/50 g):

Pattern Color ID	Color Swatch	Color ID	Color Name	Where Used	# Balls
A		184	Celedon	Border	2
B		165	Scree	Sky	2
C		227	Sorbet	Sky	2
D		185	Frozen	Sky	2
E		226	Mint	Sky	2
F		197	Alabaster	Sky	2
G		220	Sulfur	House	2
H		181	Mineral	House	1
I		223	Tango	House	1
J		198	Zinnia	House	1
K		186	Tawny	House	1
L		200	Barbara	House	1
M		199	Pink Bliss	House	1
N		161	Avocado	House/Tree	1
O		204	Vaseline Green	House/Tree	1
P		203	Electric Green	House/Tree	1
Q		152	Watery	House	1
R		215	Ceil	House	2
S		214	Ultramarine	House	1
T		151	Bilberry	House	1
U		183	Peony	House	1
V		217	Astor	House	1
W		211	Black	House	1
X		196	Barn Red	Tree/Gate	1

YARN Rowan Yarns, Alpaca Classic, DK (57% alpaca, 43% cotton; 131 yds/120 m; 0.9 oz/25 g), choosing either #184 (bright white used in sample), or #101 (a very light gray):

Pattern Color ID	Color Swatch	Color ID	Color Name	Where Used	# Balls
Y		115	Snow Flake White	Clouds/Gate	1

NEEDLES (2) US Size 4/3.5 mm 40"/100 cm circular needles, (1) US Size 7/4.5 mm needle used only as the 3rd needle in a 3-needle BO, (4) US Size 4/3.5 mm dpns, (2) US Size 0/2 mm straight needles

NOTIONS Tapestry needle, stitch markers, needle protectors, stitch holders or scrap yarn

GAUGE 20 sts x 40 rows = 4"/10 cm in garter st, with yarn held single, on US Size 4/3.5 mm or size to obtain gauge.

NOTES

- The blanket is worked in Blocks, sewn together into horizontal Strips, which are knitted together using pu&k and a 3-needle BO. Borders are added via pu&k.

- House Blocks have Windows and Doors that are worked using a combination of intarsia and fair-isle techniques. See this video to learn the technique. A House Block is composed of a Roof and a Building, worked in that order. The Roof includes the Sky.

- Other Blocks include: Carport, Trees, a Garden and Lamppost.

- Embellishments, worked separately, are sewn on.

- Blocks are 66 ridges/sts tall, and 13, 26 or 39 sts wide.

- Blocks can be worked in any order. Here are two suggested orderings:

  1. Make all the Blocks of a Strip, left-to-right or right-to-left, then do the same for remaining Strips. Attach each Block to its Strip after it is completed.

  2. Make groups of similar Blocks, such as:

     - All House Blocks of particular stitch width and Roof-type, all Tree blocks, all Lamppost blocks, all Carport blocks then all Garden blocks.

       Attach a paper label with the Block's ID, found underneath the Block in Figure 2, to each completed block. When all Blocks are complete, refer to the labels to assemble the Blocks in the correct order.

- A *knitted cast on* is recommended because it's height is equal to one row of knitting in garter stitch.

- Stitch generation, via cast on or pick up and knit, (pu&k) counts as Row 1 in this pattern. Odd-numbered rows are always on the Right Side (RS) of the work, and even-numbered rows are the Wrong Side (WS) of the work.

- Instructions say to leave long tails for sewing on right edges of Blocks, cutting all left edge tails to a weave-in length of 6"/15 cm.

- When encountering a marker during knitting, slip it unless directions say otherwise.

- To reduce the number of yarn ends to weave in:

  - Drape yarn slightly loosely to the next use whenever a pu&k will occur later on that edge, then weave in the draped yarn during the pu&k.

  - Weave-in as you are knitting a RS row by inserting the working needle under the end, every other stitch.

- Scraps of worsted or aran weight yarn work better than rigid stitch holders. A large removable stitch marker can be used to hold up to 6 stitches.

Printing Instructions

Print this pattern 2-sided (flip on long edge) if your printer has this capability, then split the pages into *booklets*, stapling each booklet together along the left margin in several places. Having separate booklets allows you to have more than one page open at a time.

The starting page number for each *booklet* is:

The pages at the end of the pattern (starting at page 46) are photo tutorials for techniques and do not need to be printed.

If your printer doesn't support 2-sided, print 1-sided and staple or glue-stick the blank sides of pairs of pages together so printed sides face out, then organize into booklets.

PATTERN RESOURCES

Tutorials

These videos, hosted on YouTube, have been created to help you with specific parts of this pattern:

Click for videos made for this pattern,

These videos demonstrate knitting techniques:

Click for knitting technique tutorials.

Yarn Kits

Jimmy Beans Wool is offering yarn kits for this blanket.

Community

Join the Facebook Knit A-Long (KAL) for this pattern. This is a private group for seeking inspiration, sharing knowledge and access to live Zoom meetups. This group will continue after the KAL is complete, with links to recorded Zoom meetups. Membership is based on answering some common knitting questions correctly. I am always looking for help moderating this group, so if you are interested, please let me know.

Contributing

This is a paid pattern. Additional design contributions from knitters are encouraged. Design contributions are freely shared. To learn how you can contribute, go to the Blanket's web page, and scroll down to the 3rd section.

UNDERSTANDING CONSTRUCTION DIAGRAMS

Blocks have written instructions that refer to one or more construction diagrams for showing how to create the pieces and connect them.

Symbols used on construction diagrams are defined below. The example on the right illustrates how the symbols are used.

Symbols used on Construction Figures

⟶	Work grows in this direction
- - - - - -	Paired increases/decreases are made around this line
▬ ▬ ▬ ▪	Sew together
▲▲▲▲▲▲	Pu&k, working on RS and starting at Colored triangle
•——•	Stitches are on holder here
⌒⌒⌒⌒⌒⌒	3-needle BO
❶ ❷ ❸	Work in this order
M	Generate M sts via pu&k or CO
N	Work N ridges, where a ridge equals 2 row, And CO or pu&k counts as 1 row.
a b c	Marked locations on construction figures
(AB)	Work this area in color AB that is specified on Figure 1.
⌄⌄⌄⌄⌄ ↑ ⌢⌢⌢⌢⌢	BO CO
⌒⌒⌒	Drape yarn loosely to next use

Example:

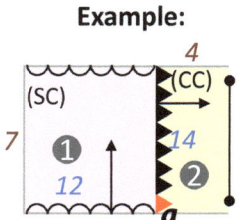

Step 1

With color SC, CO 12 sts and knit 7 ridges.
*Since CO counts as a Row, this is
(7 ridges × 2 rows/ridge) − 1 row = 13 rows.
BO.*

Step 2

With Color CC, and starting at red triangle, pu&k 14 sts to end of edge and knit 4 ridges.
*Since pu&k counts as a Row, this is
(4 ridges × 2 rows/ridge) − 1 row = 7 rows.*
Place 14 sts on holder

CONSTRUCTION OF HOUSE BLOCKS

House Blocks are the dominant Block type in this blanket.

- Figure 2 (page 5) specifies the quantities to make, type, colors and other details of House Blocks.

- House Blocks have 2 parts: a Roof and a Building, worked in that order.

- There are multiple Roof types, summarized in Table 1 on page 8. Roofs include the Sky for the block.

- Buildings come in 3 heights: 1-story, 2-story and 3-story (1S, 2S, and 3S specified on the upper left corner of a Building in Figure 2). Buildings also come in 3 widths: 13, 26, and 39 sts.

To make a House Block, work these 2 Steps:

Step 1: Roof

Work [<Roof type>] where *Roof type* is specified in the roof area of the House Block in Figure 2. Instructions for Roofs start on page 8. *Reminder:* The Sky is a part of the Roof.

Step 2: Building

Work [<Building type>]. The Building type is a combination of its width (13, 26, and 39), specified above the Block in Figure 2, and it's height (1S, 2S, or 3S) specified at the top-left corner of the Building. Instructions for House types start on page 16.

Figure 2 includes the colors for all parts of House Blocks: window frames, windowpanes, etc, for Window and Doors. The example on page 4 illustrates how to interpret the information in Figure 2.

Table of Contents (TOC)

When viewing this pattern on an electronic device, Use links, such as those below, to move between different sections of the pattern quickly. Links named "TOC" will bring you back to this page.

> *Hint:* Stay organized by crossing out completed Blocks in Figure 2.

Example: Block 5.1 in Figure 2

The house is 2-story as indicated by "2S" in the upper-left corner of the Building. The Sky color is B, specified in round braces after the "Strip 2" label. The roof-type is SL-26 worked in color T. Colors are:

Roof: T; Building: V; Window Frame: M; Windowpane: T; Door Frame: M; Door Panes: T.

The directions, if they were fully written out, would be:

Work Roof type SL-26, using T for Roof and B for Sky,
Work [2S] using V for Building, M for Window Frame, T for Windowpane, M for Door Frame and T for Door Panes.

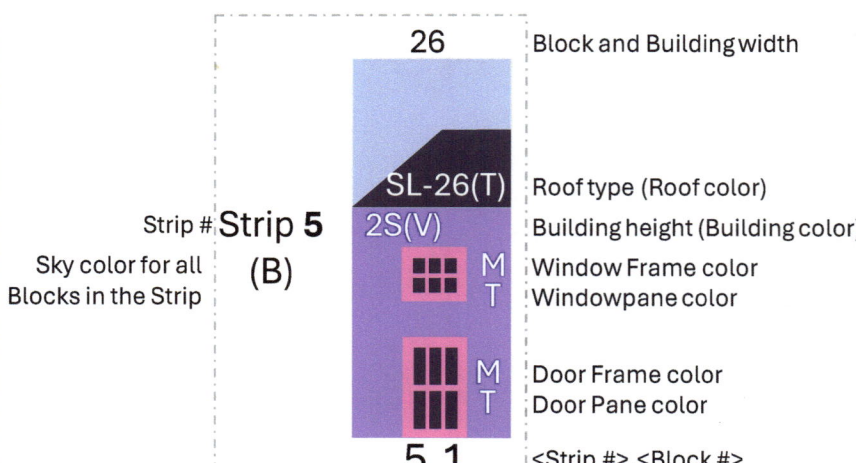

Figure 1: How to Interpret Figure 2

Color Abbreviations

A	B	C	D	E	F	G	H	I	J	K	L	M	N	O	P	Q	R	S	T	U	V	W	X	Y

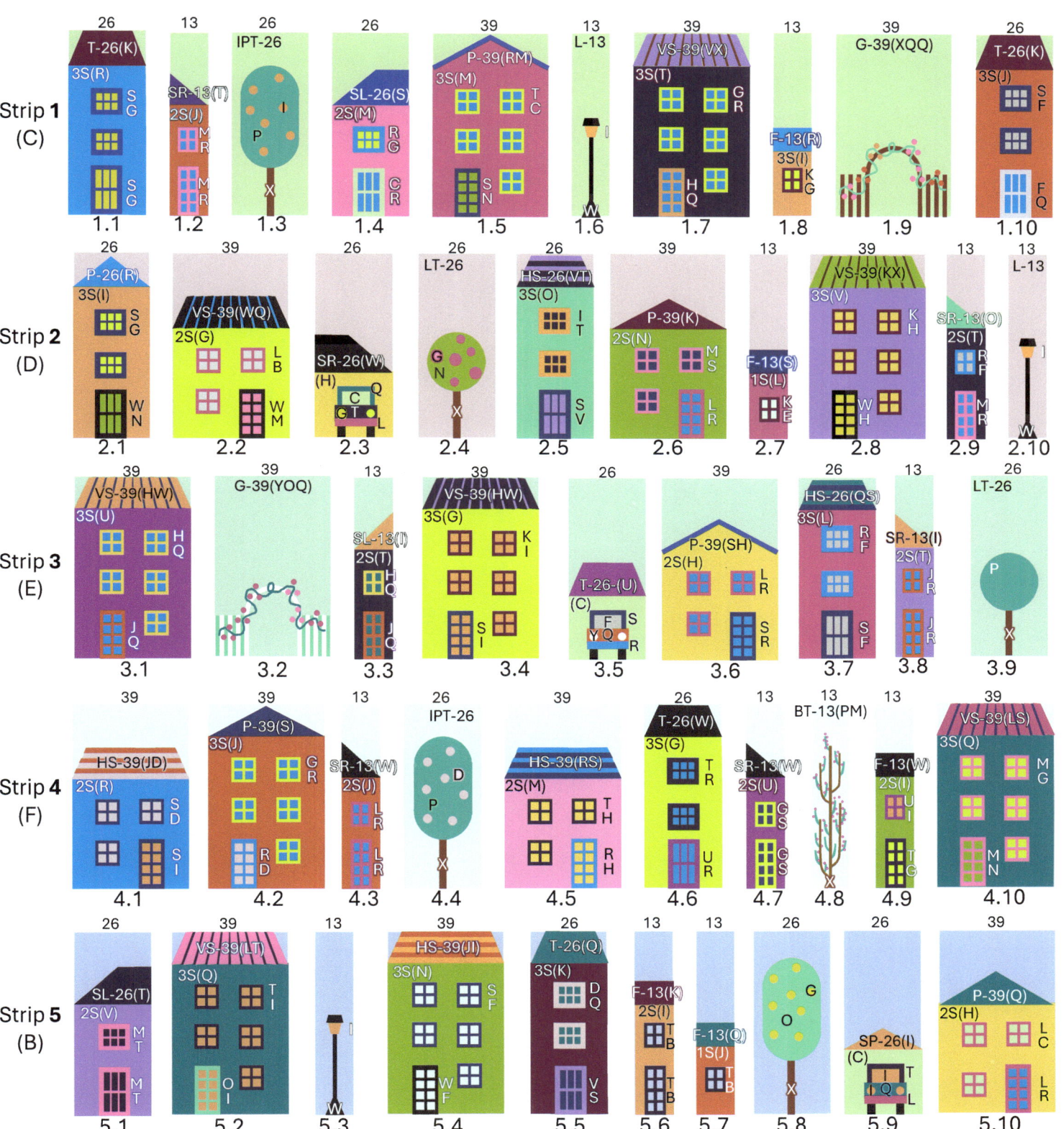

Figure 2: Blocks: Quantities, Types and Colors

This page has been intentionally left blank.

ROOFS

ROOFS

The Roof types are summarized in Table 1.

- Roofs include parts worked in the color of the Sky for the Strip.
- The order of working parts may be Roof then Sky, or Sky then Roof.
- *Reminder:* Stitch generation counts as Row 1.
-

Table 1: Roof Types

Roof Type	Block/House Width, in sts		
	13	**26**	**39**
Vertical **S**triped			VS-39
Horizontal **St**riped		HS-26	HS-39
Peaked		P-26	P-39
Truncated		T-26	
Shallow **P**eaked		SP-26	
Sloped	SR-13 / SL-13	SR-26 / SL-26	
Flat		■	

Flat Roof

Roof

With color for Roof, CO 13 sts. Knit 15 rows (8 ridges).

Turn to RS, and count to confirm there are 8 ridges.

> *Hint:* When RS is facing up, the CO tail and working yarn are hanging off the right edge.

Cut yarn leaving 12"/30 cm tail for sewing.

Sky

Continuing with color for Sky,

- **1S:** Knit 72 rows/36 ridges,
- **2S:** Knit 40 rows/20 ridges

Place sts on holder. Cut yarn leaving a tail of length:

- **1S:** 30"/75 cm,
- **2S:** 15"/40 cm.

Cont at 13 st Building.

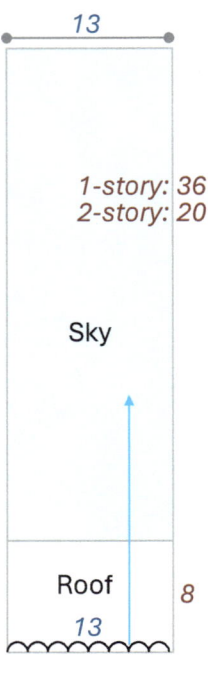

Figure 4: Flat Roof Construction

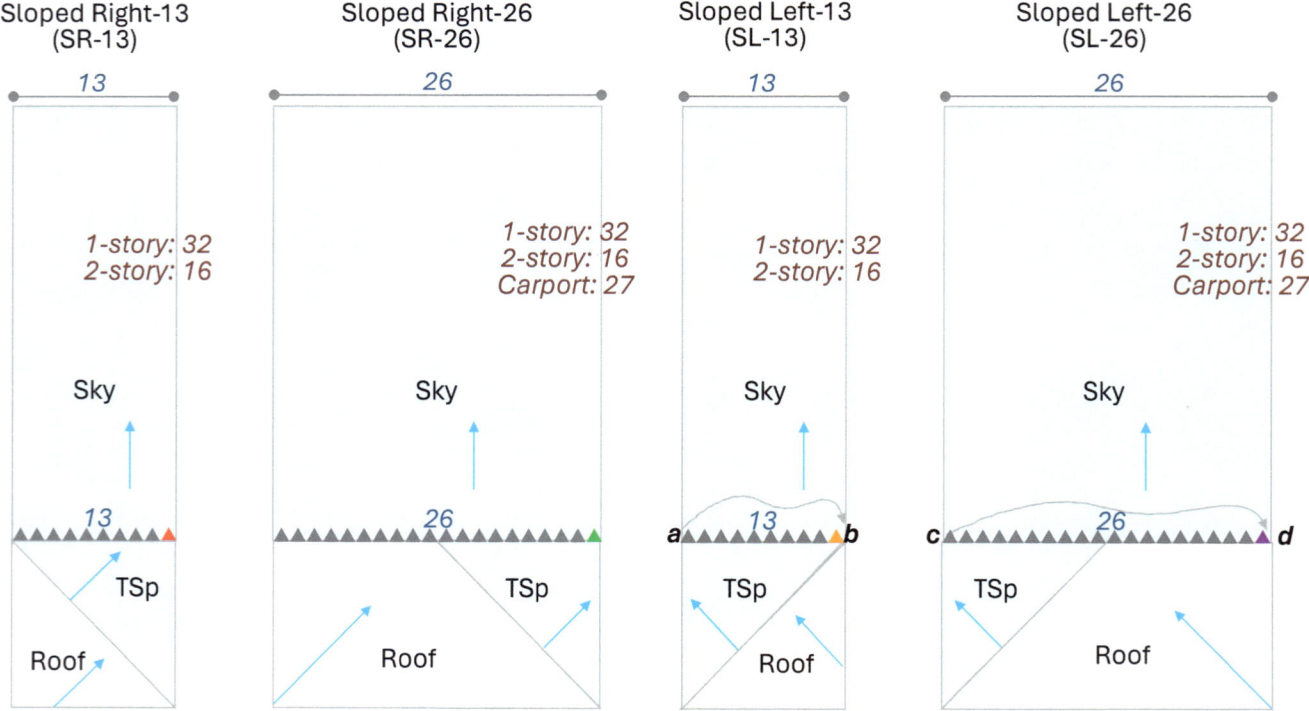

Figure 3: Construction for the 4 Types of Sloped Roofs

Sloped Roofs - SR-13, SR-26, SL-13, and SL-26

- There are 4 Sloped Roof variations, allowing Roofs to slope either right or left, and to be made to fit a 13 or 26 st-wide Block.
- See Figure 3, on page 12, for construction.

Work [Sloped Roof]. Turn to RS.

Continue at desired Sloped Roof, below.

Sloped Right-13 (SR-13)

Orient piece so fasten off is at top-right corner. Starting at the red triangle, with SC, pu&k 13 sts along edge.

Pu&k cadence: There are 9 ridges, so cadence for pu&k is:

{bump, bump, leg} twice, bump, leg, bump, bump, leg, bump, bump.

1S: Knit 31 ridges (63 rows)
2S: Knit 16 ridges (32 rows).

Place sts on holder.

Sloped Right-26 (SR-26)

Orient piece so fasten off is at top-right corner. Starting at green triangle, with SC, pu&k 26 sts along edge.

Tip: There are 18 ridges, so cadence for pu&k is:

{bump, bump, leg} 8 times, bump, bump.

1S: Knit 31 ridges (63 rows).
2S: Knit 16 ridges (32 rows).

Place sts on holder.

Sloped Left-13 (SL-13)

Orient piece so fasten off is at top-left corner, labeled *a* in Figure. Drape SC yarn slightly loosely from *a* to *b*. Starting at gold triangle at *b*, pu&k 13 sts from *b* to *a*, using pu&k cadence from SR-13.

1S: Knit 31 ridges (63 rows)
2S: Knit 16 ridges (32 rows).

Place sts on holder.

Sloped Left-26 (SL-26)

Orient piece so fasten off is at top-left corner (labeled *c* in Figure). Drape SC yarn slightly loosely from *c* to *d*. Starting at the purple triangle at *d*, pu&k 26 sts from *d* to *c*, using pu&k cadence from SR-26.

1S: Knit 31 ridges (63 rows)
2S: Knit 16 ridges (32 rows).

Place sts on holder.

Cont at 13 st Building or 26 st Building.

Sloped Roof - for Roof Types: SR-13, SL-13, SR-26, SL-26

Roof

With color for Roof, CO 1 st.
Row 2 (WS): Knit.
Row 3 (RS): Kyok – 2 sts inc'd; 3 sts.
Row 4: Knit.
Row 5: Kf&b, knit to the last st, kf&b – 2 sts inc'd; 5 sts. Mark the RS of work.
Row 6: Knit.
Rows 7-18: Rep [Rows 5 & 6] 6 more times – 12 sts inc'd; 17 sts.

SR-13 and SL-13, only

Knit 2 rows (adds 1 ridge).

SR-26 and SL-26, only

Odd-numbered rows 19-35: Rep [Ext Row] 9 times.
   Ext Row for **SR-26:** Kf&b, knit to last st, ssk.
   Ext Row for **SL-26:** K2tog, knit to last st, kf&b.
Note: Adds 9 more ridges.

Triangular Sky part (TSp in Figure 3) for all Roof Types

Dec row (RS): With color for Sky, k2tog, knit to the last 2 sts, ssk – 2 sts dec'd; 15 sts.
Plain row (WS): Knit.
Rep [Dec row & Plain row] 6 more times – 12 sts dec'd; 3 sts.

Next RS row: Cdd – 2 sts dec'd; 1 st. Fasten off by enlarging the last st on needle and inserting yarn ball through loop and tighten. Do not cut yarn.

Truncated Roof, T-26 See Figure 5 for construction.

Roof

With color for Roof, CO 39 sts. Pm after 13th and 26th sts.

Work [T-26].

Turn piece RS-up, and orient as shown in Figure 5.

Truncated Roof (T-26) – 39 dec'ing to 1 st

Note: The number 26 in the name of this shape indicates the width of the final shape, expressed in sts.
Rows 2 (WS) to 4: Knit.
Row 5 (RS): K2tog, *knit to 2 sts bef next m, ssk, k2tog; rep from * once more; knit to last 2 sts, ssk – 6 sts dec'd; 33 sts.
Row 6: Knit.
Row 7: Rep [Row 5] – 6 sts dec'd; 27 sts.
Rows 8-13: Rep [Rows 2-7] once – 12 sts dec'd; 15 sts.
Rows 14-18: Rep [Rows 2-6] once – 6 sts dec'd; 9 sts.
Rows 19 (RS) & 20 (WS): Knit.
Row 21: Cdd 3 times – 6 sts dec'd; 3 sts.
Row 22: Cdd once – 2 sts dec'd; 1 st.
Cut yarn and fasten off.

HLp

Starting at green triangle, with color for Sky, pu&k 12 sts to next corner Work [HLp, on page 12]. Cut yarn and fasten off, leaving 10"/25 cm tail.

HRp

Starting at yellow triangle, pu&k 12 sts to next corner. Work [HRp, on page 12]. To fasten off, enlarge last st, insert ball through and tighten.

3S: Cut yarn leaving 10"/25 cm tail. Roof is complete.
1S and 2S: Do not cut yarn.

Sky

With yarn still attached, and starting at purple triangle, pu&k 26 sts along top edge to next corner (7 sts on edge of HRp, 13 sts on edge of T-26 and 6 sts on edge of HLp).

1S: Knit 63 rows/32 ridges.
2S: Knit 31 rows/16 ridges.

Place sts on holder.

1S: Cut yarn leaving 30"/75 cm.
2S: Cut yarn leaving 20"/50 cm.

Cont at 26 st Building.

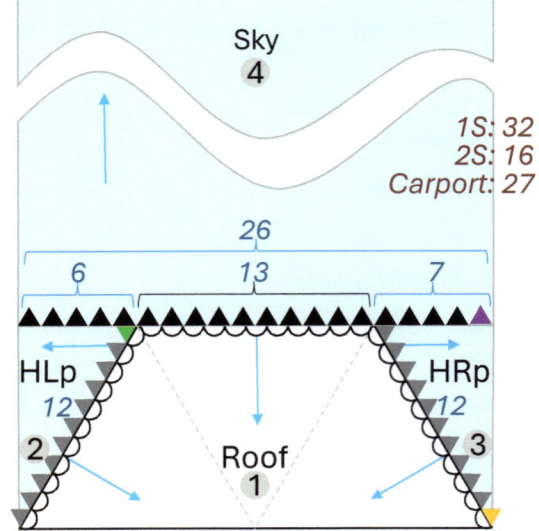

Figure 5: Truncated Roof, T-26, construction

Peaked Roof - P-39 See Figure 6 for construction.

Sky With color for Sky,

2S: CO 28 sts.
3S: CO 13 sts.

Work [PS-39].

> **Peaked Sky 39 (PS-39)** – 28 (13) sts dec'ing to 18 (3) sts inc'ing to 28 (12) sts

Note 1: Directions are for the 2S Building with changes for the 3S in brackets.
Row 2 (WS): Knit.
Row 3 (RS): K2tog, knit to end – 1 st dec'd; 27 (12) sts.
Rows 4-6: Knit; 3 ridges complete.
Rows 7-38: Rep [Rows 3-6] 8 times – 8 sts dec'd; 19 (4) sts; 19 ridges complete.
Row 39: Rep [Row 3] – 1 st dec'd; 18 (3) sts.
Row 40: Knit. Pm on R edge of 20th ridge.
Row 41: Kf&b, knit to end – 1 st inc'd; 19 (4) sts.
Rows 42-44: Knit; 22 ridges complete.
Rows 45-76: Rep [Rows 41-44] 8 times – 8 sts inc'd; 27 (12) sts; 38 ridges complete.
Row 77: Rep [Row 41] – 1 st inc'd; 28 (13) sts.
Row 78: Knit. BO loosely. Cut yarn and fasten off, leaving 30"/75 cm tail.

Roof

Turn piece RS-up. With color for Roof, and starting at red triangle, pu&k 21 to corner, 1 st in corner, pm, pu&k 21 to next corner – 43 sts. Work [PR-39].

> **Peaked Roof 39 (PR-39)** – 43 sts dec'ing 1 st

Row 2 (WS): K2tog, knit to last 2 sts, ssk – 2 sts dec'd; 41 sts.
Row 3: K2tog, knit to 2 sts bef m, rm, cdd, pm, knit to last 2 sts, ssk – 4 sts dec'd; 37 sts
Rows 4-6: Rep [Row 2] 3 times – 6 sts dec'd; 31 sts.
Rows 7-14: Rep [Rows 3-6] 2 times – 20 sts dec'd; 11 sts.
Row 15: Rep [Row 3] once – 4 sts dec'd; 7 sts.
Rows 16 & 17: Rep [Row 2] twice – 4 sts dec'd; 3 sts.
Row 18: Cdd – 2 sts dec'd; 1 st. Cut yarn and fasten off.

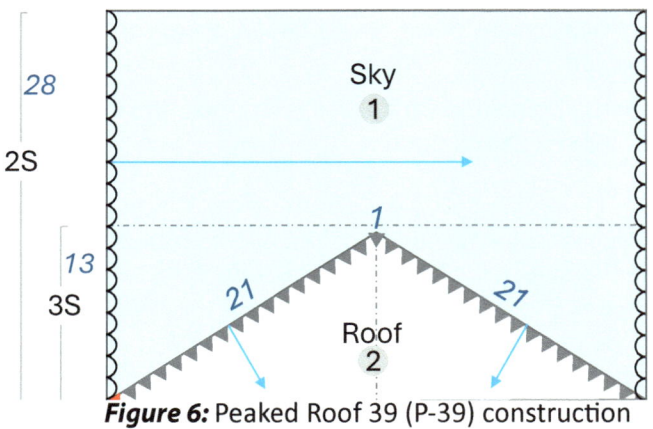

Figure 6: Peaked Roof 39 (P-39) construction

Cont at 9 st Building.

Peaked Roof - P-26 See Figure 7 for construction.

Sky With color for Sky,

2S: CO 28 sts.
3S: CO 12 sts.

Work [PS-26].

> **Peaked Sky 26 (PS-26)** – 28 (13) sts dec'ing to 18 (3) sts inc'ing to 28 (13) sts

Note 1: Directions are for the 2S Building with changes for the 3S in brackets.
Note 2: St generation counts as Row 1.
All Shapes:
Row 2: Knit.
Row 3: K2tog, knit to end – 1 st dec'd; 27 (12) sts.
Rows 4: Knit.
Rows 5-26: Rep [Rows 3 & 4] 11 times – 11 sts dec'd; 16 (1) sts.
Row 27: Kf&b, knit to end – 1 st inc'd; 17 (2) sts.
Row 28: Knit.
Rows 31-52: Rep [Rows 27 & 28] 11 times – 11 sts inc'd; 28 (13) sts.
Cut yarn, leaving 30"/75 cm (15"/40 cm) tail. Fasten off.

Roof

Turn piece RS-up. With color for Roof, and starting at red triangle, pu&k 17 to corner, 1 st in corner, pm, 17 to next corner – 35 sts. Work [PR-26].

> **Peaked Roof 26 (PR-26)** – 35 sts dec'ing 1 st

Row 2 and all even-numbered (WS) to18: Knit.
Row 3: K2tog, knit to 2 sts bef m, rm, cdd, pm, knit to last 2 sts, ssk – 4 sts dec'd; 31 sts
Rows 4-17: Rep [Rows 2 & 3] 7 more times – 28 sts dec'd; 3 sts.
Row 19: Cdd – 2 sts dec'd; 1 st. Cut yarn and fasten off.

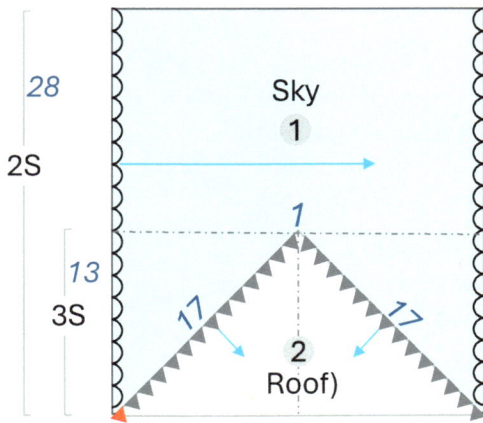

Figure 7: Peaked Roof 26 (P-26) - construction

Cont at 26 st Building.

Horizontal Striped Roof 26 (39); HS-26 (HS-39)

- See Figure 8 for construction.
- Color "C1" is the color used for CO. Color "C2" is the color for alternate stripes.
- Instructions in this section are for HS-26 with changes for HS-39 in parentheses.

Roof

With C1, CO 14 (27) sts. Work [Horizontal Striped Roof].

> **Horizontal Striped Roof 26 (39) (HS-26 (HS-39)** - 14 (27) sts inc'ing to 26 (39) sts

Drape yarn bet uses on right edge of shape.

Rows 2 (WS): Cont with C1, knit.
Row 3 (RS): Kf&b, knit to last st, kf&b – 2 sts inc'd; 16 (29) sts.
Row 4: Knit. Drop C1 but do not cut.
Rows 5 & 6: With C2, knit.
Rows 7 & 8: Rep [Rows 3 & 4] 2 sts inc'd; 18 (31) sts. Drop C2, but do not cut.
Row 9: Knit.
Rows 10-24: Rep [Rows 2-9] twice, ending 2nd rep after Row 8 – 8 sts inc'd; 26 (39) sts. Cut yarns and fasten off.

HLp

Turn piece RS-up and orient as shown. With color for Sky, starting at green triangle at top-left corner of the Roof, pu&k 12 sts to corner (1 st per garter st ridge). Work [HLp].

> **Hex Left piece (HLp)** - 12 sts

Row 2 and all even-numbered (WS) rows to 12: Knit.
Row 3. K1, w&t.
Row 5: K3, w&t.
Row 7: K5, w&t.
Row 9: K7, w&t.
Row 11: K9, w&t.
BO loosely. Cut yarn, leaving 15"/40 cm tail, fasten off.

HRp

With color for Sky, and starting at red triangle at the bottom-right corner of the Roof, pu&k 12 sts to corner (1 st per garter st ridge). Work [HRp].

> **Hex Right piece (HRp)** - 12 sts

Row 2 (WS): K1, w&t.
Row 3 and all RS rows to 11: Knit.
Row 4: K3, w&t.
Row 6: K5, w&t.
Row 8: K7, w&t.
Row 10: K9, w&t.
After completing RS Row 11, BO loosely.
BO loosely. Cut yarn, leaving 15"/40 cm tail, fasten off.

Do not cut yarn. Enlarge last loop and insert yarn ball through and tighten.

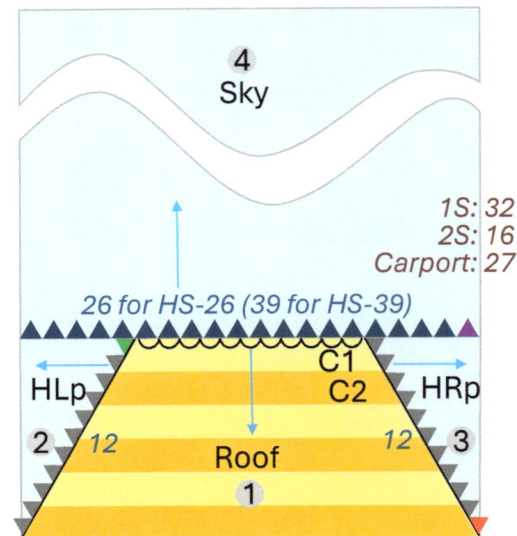

Figure 8: Horizontal Striped Roofs 26, 39 (HS-26, HS-39)

Sky

2S: With yarn still attached, and starting purple triangle, pu&k 26 (39) sts to corner (6 sts on Hrp, 14 (27) sts on HS, and 6 sts on Hlp). Knit 31 rows/16 ridges. Place sts on holder. Cut yarn leaving 20"/50 cm tail. Roof is complete.

3S: Cut yarn. Roof is complete.

Cont at 26 st Building or 39 st Building.

Vertical Striped Roof 39 (VS-39)

See Figure 9 on page 13 for construction.

Roof

With MC, CO 13 sts. Work [VS-39] on page 13, or work from VS-39 Chart.

Turn piece RS-up and orient as shown in Figure 9.

Hlp

With color for Sky, and starting at the green triangle at the top-left corner of the Roof, pu&k 12 sts to corner (1 st per CO st).

Work [Hlp]. Cut yarn, leaving 15"/30 cm tail, and fasten off.

Hrp

With color for Sky, and starting at the red triangle at the bottom-right corner of the Roof, pu&k 12 sts to corner (1 st per CO st).

Work [Hrp]. Do not cut yarn. Enlarge last loop and insert yarn ball through and tighten.

Sky

2S: With yarn still attached from Hrp, and starting at the purple triangle, pu&k 39 sts to next corner (6 sts on the top edge of Hrp, 27 sts on the top edge of the Roof, and 6 sts on the top edge of Hlp). Knit 31 rows/16 ridges. Place sts on holder. Cut yarn leaving 20"/50 cm tail. Roof is complete.

3S: Cut yarn. Roof is complete.

Vertical Striped Roof -39 (VS-39) – 13 sts dec'ing to 12 sts inc'ing to 13 sts

Row 2 and all even-numbered (WS) rows to 74: Knit, in same color as prev RS row.

MC | **Row 3 (RS):** K2tog, k4, w&t – 1 st dec'd; 12 sts.

C1 | **Rows 5:** Knit to last st, kf&b – 1 st inc'd; 13 sts.

   | **Row 7:** Knit.

MC | **Row 9:** K2tog, k5, w&t – 1 st dec'd; 12 sts.

   | **Row 11:** Knit.

C1 | **Row 13:** Knit to last st, kf&b – 1 st inc'd; 13 sts.

Rows 15, 17, 19, and 21: Rep Rows 7, 9, 11, and 13.

Rows 23, 25, 27, and 29: Rep Rows 7, 9, 11, and 13, omitting kf&b at end of Row 13 – 1 st dec'd; 12 sts.

   | **Row 31:** Knit.

MC | **Row 33:** K7, w&t.

   | **Row 35:** Knit.

C1 | **Row 37:** Knit.

Rows 39, 41, 43, and 45: Rep Rows 31, 33, 35, and 37.

   | **Row 47:** Knit.

MC | **Row 49:** Kf&b, k5, w&t – 1 st inc'd; 13 sts.

   | **Row 51:** Knit.

C1 | **Row 53:** Knit.

   | **Row 55:** Knit to last 2 sts, ssk – 1 st dec'd; 12 sts.

MC | **Row 57:** Kf&b, k5, w&t – 1 st inc'd; 13 sts.

   | **Row 59:** Knit.

Rows 61, 63, 65, and 67: Rep Rows 53, 55, 57, and 59.

C1 | **Row 69:** Knit.

   | **Row 71:** K5, w&t.

MC | **Row 73:** Kf&b, knit to last 2 sts, ssk.

   | BO loosely (after WS Row 74). Cut yarns and fasten off.

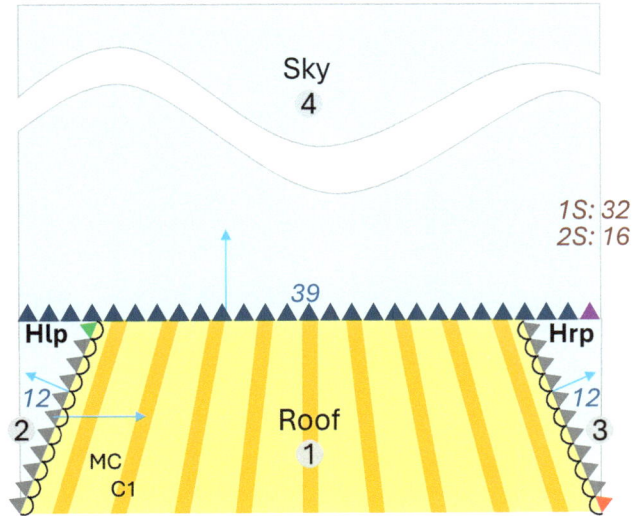

Figure 9: Vertical Striped Roof 39 (VS-39) construction

Note: When working a pu&k on the bottom edge of a VS type roof, simultaneously weave in draped yarns.

Cont at 39 st Building.

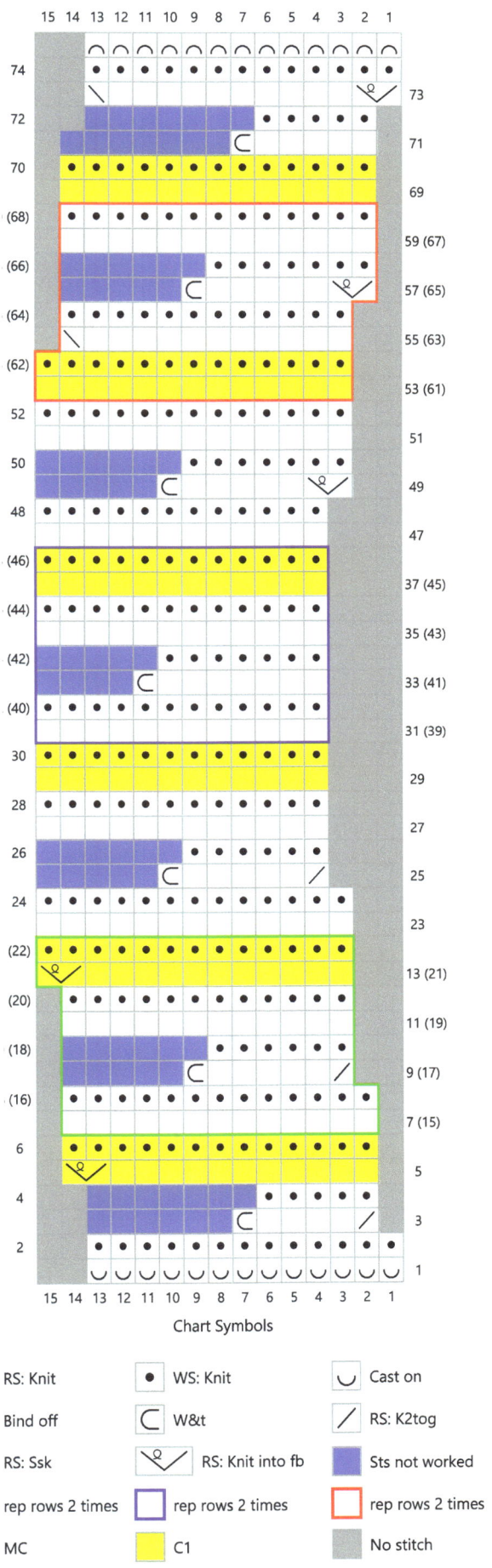

VS-39 Chart

Chart Symbols

RS: Knit	• WS: Knit	⌣ Cast on
⌢ Bind off	C W&t	╱ RS: K2tog
╲ RS: Ssk	⌿ RS: Knit into fb	Sts not worked
rep rows 2 times (green)	rep rows 2 times (purple)	rep rows 2 times (red)
MC	C1	No stitch

Shallow Peaked Roof 26 (SP-26)- see Figure 10

Notes

SP-26 on a Carport

Work Carport (page 28) first.

On the top edge of the Carport, with color for Roof, pu&k 26 sts (1 per BO st) bet corner m's.

SP-26 on a 2S or 3S Building

Work SP-26 first. To generate sts, with color for Roof, CO 26 sts. When working the Building generate sts via pu&k on the bottom (cast on) edge of SP-26.

Roof

Generate 26 sts in color for Roof (see *Notes* above), work [SP-26].

> **Shallow Peaked 26 (SP-26)** – 26 sts dec'ing to 1 st

Row 1: K2tog, knit to last 2 sts, ssk – 2 sts dec'd.
Rep [Row 1] 24 more times – 24 sts dec'd; 1 st.
Cut yarn and fasten off.

Double Triangle (DT)

Starting at the green triangle at **a**, on the right corner of SP-26 with SC, pu&k 14 sts evenly to peak of SP-26, and 14 sts from yellow triangle to **b**. Work [DT].

> **Double Triangle (DT)** – 26 sts

Row 2 (WS):K2, w&t.
Row 3 and all even-numbered (RS) rows to 11: Knit.
Row 4: K4, w&t.
Row 6: K6, w&t.
Row 8: K8, w&t.
Row 10: K10, w&t.
Row 12 (WS): Knit to end.
RS Rows 13, 15, 17, 19, 21: Rep Rows 2, 4, 6, 8, and 10.
WS Rows 14, 16, 18, 20 and 22: Knit. Do not cut yarn.

Sky

Carport: Knit 67 rows (34 ridges).
2S: Knit 43 rows/22 ridges.
3S: Knit 11 rows/6 ridges.

Place 26 sts on holder. Cut yarn and fasten off leaving long tail for sewing.

Cont at 26 st Building.

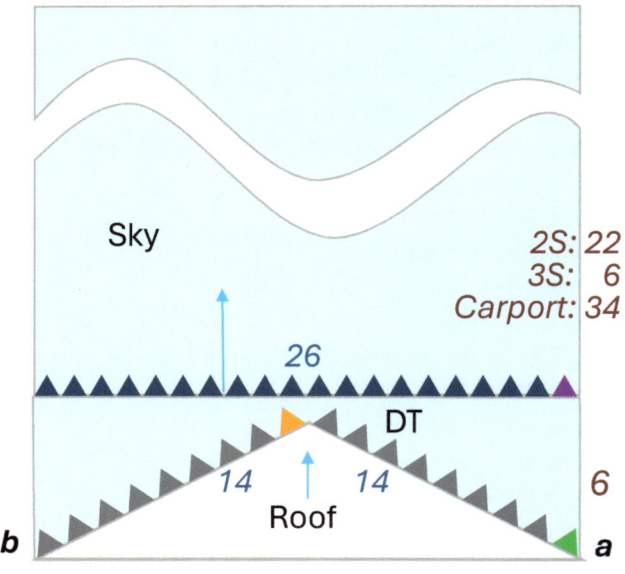

Figure 10: Construction Shallow Peaked 26 (SP-26) Roof

BUILDINGS

Recommendation for needles:

*   When working the vertical *Strips* of the Buildings (the vertical *Strips* have Windows and/or Doors), use wooden dpns. Since there are 12 or fewer stitches on the needle, the stitches won't fall off the ends, and when turning work, the yarn won't catch as much on dpns because they are shorter and do not have end caps.

*   When working the parts of a Building that have more stitches; such as Left Edge, Right Edge and Folding Rectangle; either change to straight needles or add stitch protectors to convert the wooden dpns to a straight needles.

Yarn management while working Windows and Doors:

Cut 2 yards of the Pane Color if working a Window, and slightly more if working a Door, and leave this strand loose. Work the Frame Color from the ball. When yarns tangle, pull out the strand of Pane Color to quickly and easily untangle. If running out of Pane Color, avoid more weaving in by spit-splicing on a new piece.

BUILDINGS

- Buildings come in 3 widths and 3 heights. In Figure 2 on page 5, the *height* (1S, 2S, or 3S) is specified at the top-left corner of the Building, just under the Roof. The *width* (13, 26, or 39 sts) is specified on top of the Block.

- The Roof for the Block is completed before working the Building.

- There is a construction diagram for each Building width and height combination found in Figure 2. 1S with widths 26 or 39 sts, and 3S with width 13 sts do not appear in Figure 2.

- Windows and Doors are worked from charts which are positioned near where they are referenced in the written instructions. They combine garter stitch, fair isle (aka stranded color work), and intarsia. Learn this technique by watching this video.

- Color abbreviations for Buildings are:

  BB - <u>B</u>uilding <u>B</u>ackground, used for the Header, spaces between and around Windows and Doors.
  FW - <u>F</u>rames of <u>W</u>indows. All windows in a given Building are worked in the same two colors (FW and PW).
  PW - <u>P</u>anes of <u>W</u>indows
  FD - <u>F</u>rames of <u>D</u>oors
  PD - <u>P</u>anes of <u>D</u>oors

- The vertical column starting at the top-most Window or Door is called a *Strip*. 13 st and 26 st-wide House Blocks have one Strip, and the 39 st-wide House Block has two Strips.

- In construction diagrams, the number of sts to pu&k for a Left Edge, Right Edge, or Folding Rectangle are shown in blue italics on the edge of each element of the Strip (on the edges of Window(s), Door, etc.)

Building 13

This is a 13-stitch wide Building, identified by the number "13" on top of the Block in Figure 2.

This building has two height options:

- 1-story (1S). See Figure 11 for construction.

- 2-story (2S). See Figure 12 for construction.

Header *(1st Step of Figure)*

Turn Roof piece RS-up. With BB and starting at the bottom-left corner of the Roof, at the red triangle, pu&k 13 sts evenly to corner.

Knit 11 rows (6 ridges including the pu&k). Do not cut BB.

Place first 2 sts of row on a holder, and place last 2 sts of row on a separate holder. Do not cut BB.

Strip

Beg on the RS, and continuing with the 9 center stitches still on the needle, with FW and PW, work [Window-9 chart]. Cut FW and PW.

Draping BB loosely along edge of Window, knit 10 rows (5 ridges).

1S: Place sts on holder. Cut BB.
2S: Cut BB. With FD and PD, work [Door-9 chart]. Place sts on holder. Cut yarns used for Door.

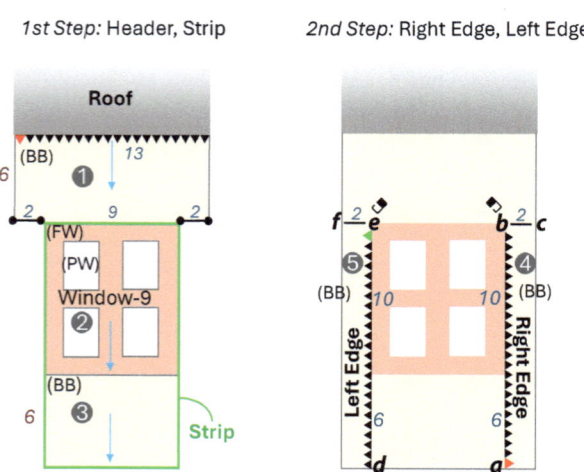

Figure 11: Building 13, 1S Construction

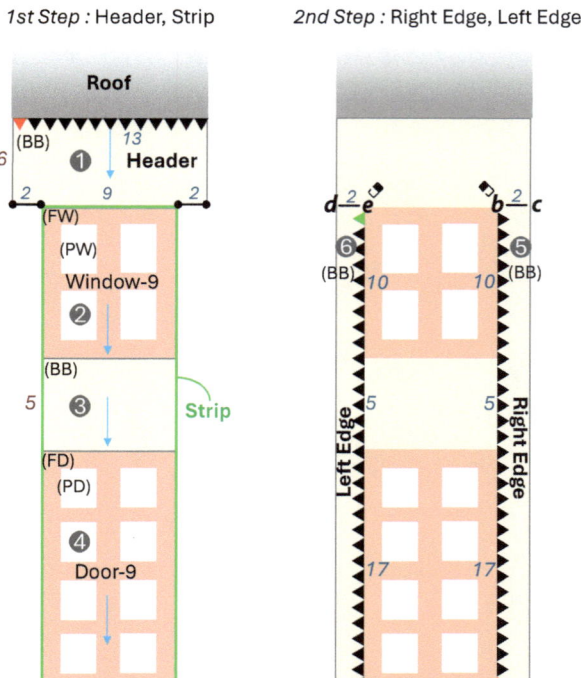

Figure 12: Building 13, 2S Construction

Right Edge (2nd Step of Figure)

With BB, and starting at the bottom-right corner of the Window/Door Strip, at the red triangle (*a*):

1S: Pu&k 16 sts to *b*, pm, knit 2 sts from holder bet *b* and *c* – 18 sts.

2S: Pu&k 32 sts to *b* (16 on Door, 6 in area worked in BC bet Door & Window, and 10 on Window), pm, knit 2 sts from holder bet *b* and *c* – 34 sts.

Work [Right Edge]. *Note:* BO is on Row 4.

Right Edge

Row 2 (WS): Knit.
Row 3 (RS). Knit to 2 sts bef m, ssk, k2tog, knit to end – 2 sts dec'd.
Row 4: Knit.
Rep [Rows 3 & 4] until 1 st rem <u>after</u> m, ending after completion of a Row 3.
Rm.
Next row (WS): K2tog, BO all sts loosely.
Cut yarns and fasten off leaving long tail for sewing.

Left Edge (2nd Step of Figure)

With BB, knit 2 sts from holder bet *d* and *e*, pm, then:

1S: Starting at green triangle (*e*), pu&k 10 sts on Window edge, and 6 sts on edge of area labeled "3" to *f* – 18 sts.

2S: Starting at green triangle (*e*), pu&k 32 sts (10 on edge of Window, 6 on edge of area labeled "3", and 16 on edge of Door) – 34 sts.

Work [Left Edge]. *Note:* BO is on Row 4.

Left Edge

Row 2 (WS): Knit.
Row 3 (RS). Knit to 2 sts bef m, ssk, k2tog, knit to end – 2 sts dec'd.
Row 4: Knit.
Rep [Rows 3 & 4] until 1 st rem <u>bef</u> m, ending after completion of a Row 3.
Rm.
Next Row (WS): BO to last 2 sts, ssk, BO last st.
Cut yarns and fasten off.

Charts

Window-9

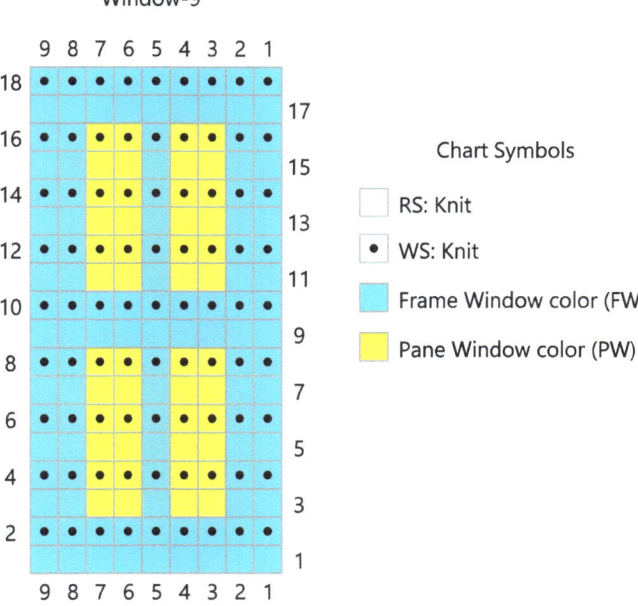

Chart Symbols

- RS: Knit
- WS: Knit
- Frame Window color (FW)
- Pane Window color (PW)

Door-9

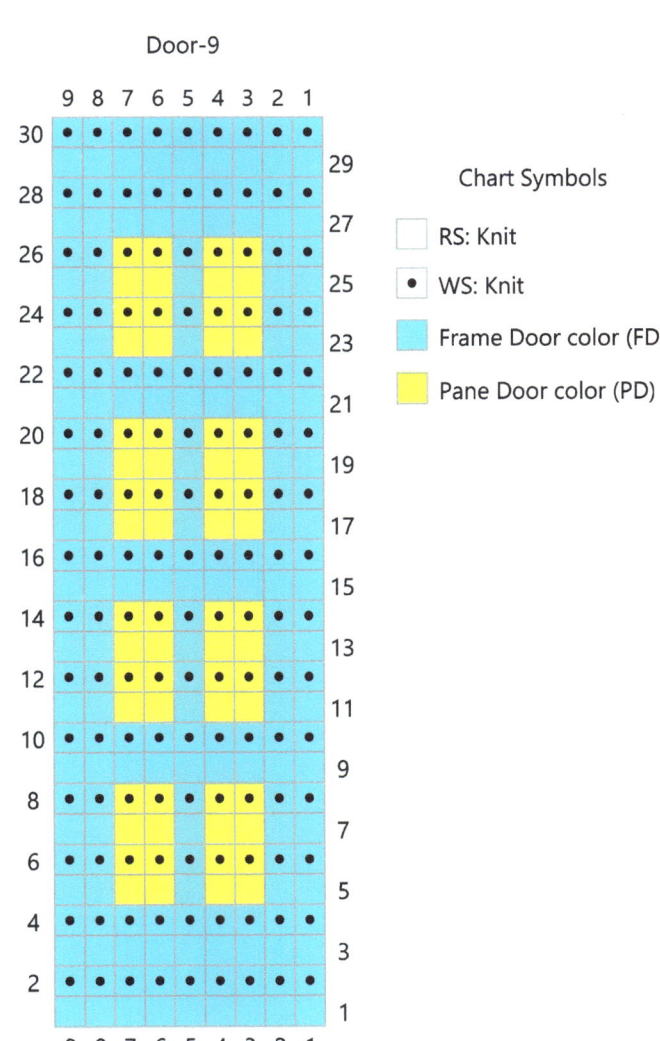

Chart Symbols

- RS: Knit
- WS: Knit
- Frame Door color (FD)
- Pane Door color (PD)

Building 26

This is a 26-stitch wide Building, identified by the number "26" on top of the Block in Figure 2.

This building has two height options:

- 2-story (2S). See Figure 13 for construction.
- 3-story (3S). See Figure 14 for construction.

Header *(1st Step of Figure)*

Turn Roof piece RS-up. With BB and starting at the bottom-left corner of the Roof, at the red triangle, pu&k 26 sts evenly to corner.

Knit 11 rows (6 ridges including the pu&k). Do not cut BB.

Place first 7 sts of row on a holder (scrap yarn), and place last 7 sts of row on a separate holder (scrap yarn).

Strip

Continuing with the rem 12 center sts still on the needle, starting on the RS, with FW and PW, work [Window-12 chart]. Cut FW and PW.

Draping BB loosely along edge of Window, knit 10 rows (5 ridges):

2S: Work [Door-12 chart]. Place sts on holder. Cut yarns for Door.

3S: Work [Window-12 chart]. Drape BB loosely along Window edge. With BB, knit 10 rows (5 ridges). Cut BB. Work [Door-12 chart]. Place sts on holder. Cut yarns for Door.

Right Edge

With BB, and starting at the red triangle at the bottom-right corner of Strip (*a*):

2S: Pu&k 32 sts on right edge of Strip bet *a* and *b*, pm, then knit 7 sts from holder bet *b* and *c* – 39 sts.

3S: Pu&k 48 sts on right edge of Strip bet *a* and *b*, pm, knit 7 sts from holder – 55 sts.

Work [Right Edge, on page 17].

Left Edge *(2nd Step of Figure)*

With BB, knit 7 sts from holder bet *d* and *e*, pm, then:

2S: Starting at green triangle (*e*), pu&k 32 sts on left edge of Strip from *e* to *f* – 39 sts.

3S: Starting at green triangle (*e*), pu&k 48 sts on left edge of Strip from *e* to *f* – 55 sts.

Work [Left Edge, on page 17].

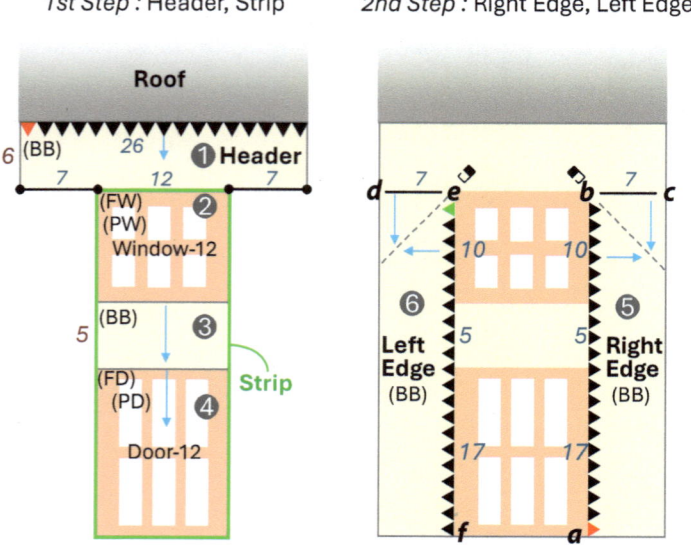

Figure 13: Building 26, 2S Construction

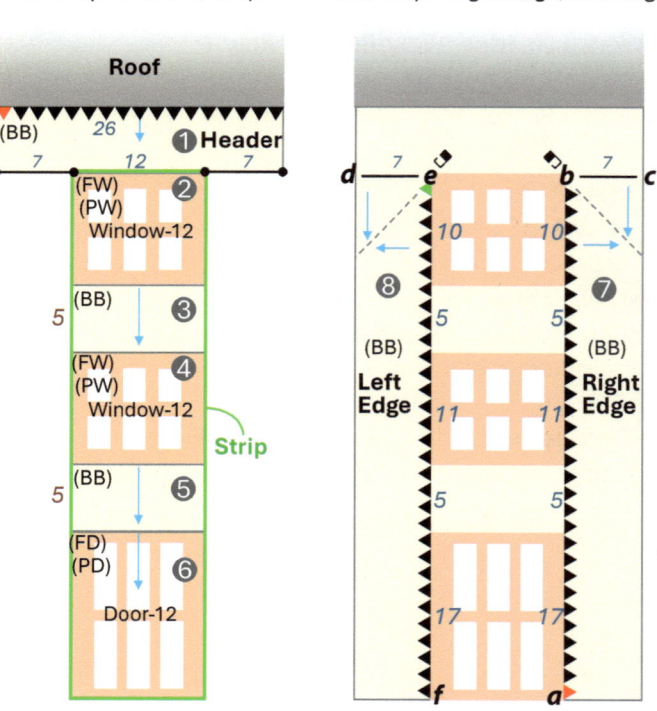

Figure 14: Building 26, 3S Construction

Charts

Window-12

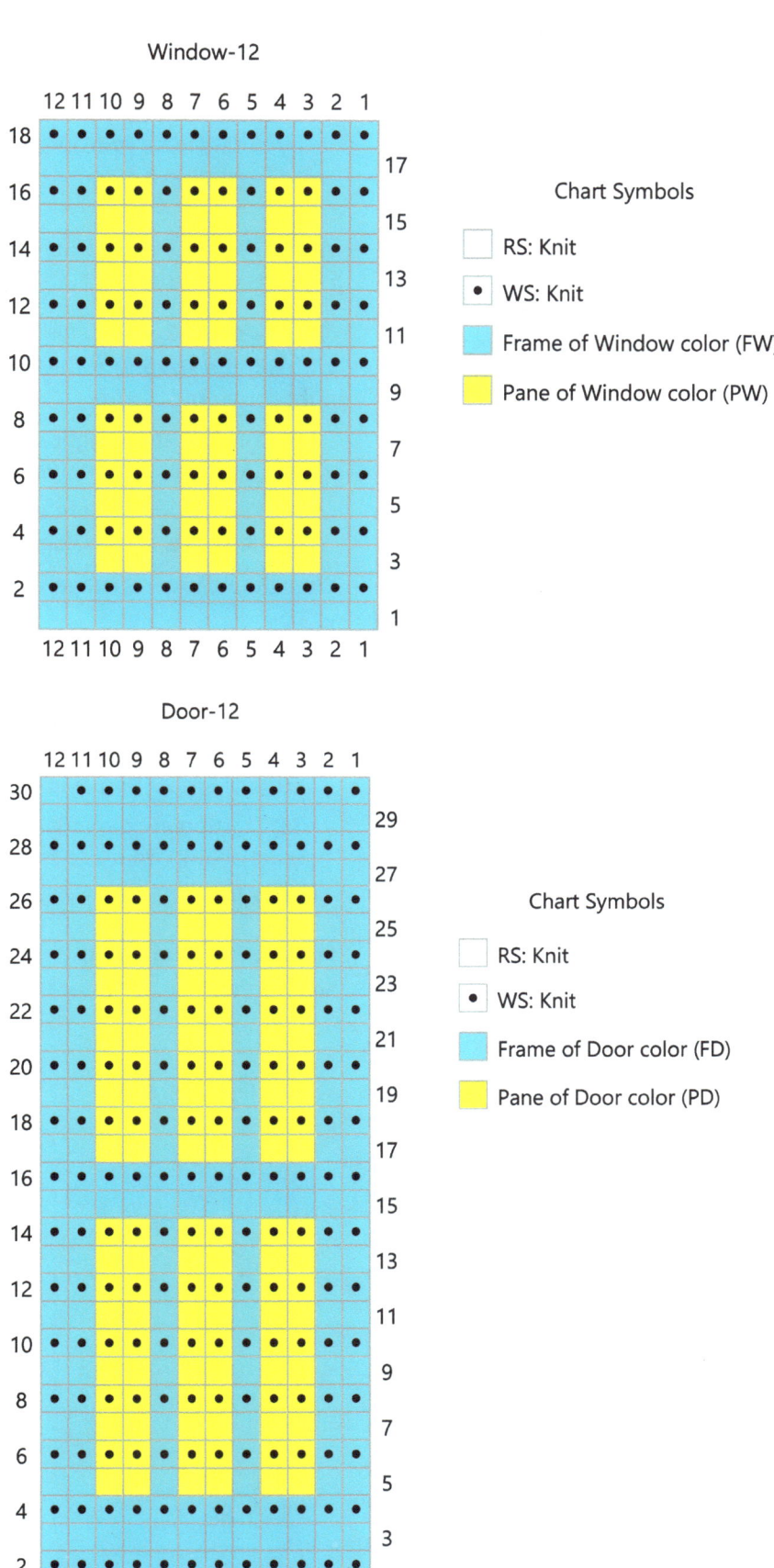

Door-12

Chart Symbols

☐ RS: Knit

• WS: Knit

🟦 Frame of Window color (FW)

🟨 Pane of Window color (PW)

Chart Symbols

☐ RS: Knit

• WS: Knit

🟦 Frame of Door color (FD)

🟨 Pane of Door color (PD)

Building 39

This is a 39-stitch wide Building, indicated by the number "39" on top of the Block in Figure 2.

This building has two height options:

- 2-story (2S). See Figure 15 for construction.
- 3-story (3S). See Figure 16 for construction.

Header (1st Step of Figure)

Turn Roof piece RS-up. With BB and starting at the bottom-left corner of the Roof, at the red triangle, pu&k 39 sts evenly to corner.

Knit 11 rows (6 ridges including the pu&k). Do not cut BB.

Turn work to RS. Separate sts into 5 Sets as follows:

- Place first 6 sts of row on holder [Set 1],
- Place next 11 sts on separate holder [Set 2],
- Place next 5 sts on a separate holder [Set 3],
- Place next 11 sts on a separate holder [Set 4], and
- Place last 6 sts on a separate holder [Set 5].

Window Strip

This is the Strip containing only Windows. For 2S this Strip is positioned on the left. For 3S it is positioned on the right.

2S: Transfer 11 sts from Set 2 to needle
3S: Transfer 11 sts from Set 4 to needle.

Note: Drape yarn loosely along edge to next use, and do not cut until instructed.

With RS of work facing, *using FW and PW, work [Window-11 chart]. Knit 10 rows (5 ridges) with BB.*

2S: Rep bet * and * once.
3S: Rep bet * and * twice.

Knit 2 more rows (1 ridge) in BB. Place sts on holders.

Door Strip

This is the Strip with a combination of Windows and a Door. For 2S this Strip is positioned on the right. For 3S it is positioned on the left.

2S: Transfer 11 sts from Set 4 to needle. Work bet * and * of *Window Strip* once. Cut FW and PW.
3S: Transfer 11 sts from Set 2 to needle. Work bet * and * of *Window Strip* twice. Cut FW and PW.

With FD and PD, work [Door-11 chart]. Cut FD and PD. Place sts on holder.

Right Edge (2nd Step of Figure)

With BB, and starting at the red triangle at the bottom-right corner of Strip (*a*):

2S: Pu&k 32 sts on right edge of Strip 2 bet *a* and *b*, pm), knit 6 sts from holder bet *b* and *c* – 39 sts.
3S: Pu&k 48 sts on right edge of Strip 1 bet *a* and *b*, pm, knit 6 sts from holder bet *b* and *c* – 54 sts.

Work [Right Edge, on page 17].

Strip 2

Left Edge

With BB, knit 6 sts from holder bet *d* and *e*, pm, then:

2S: Starting at green triangle (*e*), pu&k 32 sts on left edge of Strip 2 from *e* to *f* – 38 sts.

3S: Starting at green triangle (*e*), pu&k 48 sts on left edge of Strip from *e* to *f* – 54 sts.

Work [Left Edge, on page 17].

Folding Rectangle (FR)

See the *2nd Step* of Figure 15 (Figure 16).

With BB, and starting at purple triangle (*g*):

2S: Pu&k 32 sts on edge of *g* to *h*, pm.
3S: Pu&k 48 sts from *g* to *h*, pm.

Knit 5 sts off holder for [Set 3] bet *h* and *i*.

2S: Pu&k 32 sts from *i* to *j* – 69 sts.
3S: Pu&k 48 sts from *i* to *j* – 101 sts.

Work [Folding Rectangle, on page 21].

Step 1: Header, Strip 1, Strip 2

2nd Step : Right Edge, Left Edge, Folding Rectangle (FR)

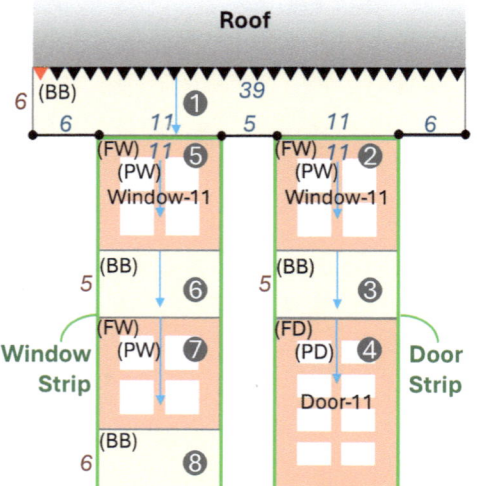

Figure 15: Building 39, 2S Construction

TOC

Charts

Window-11

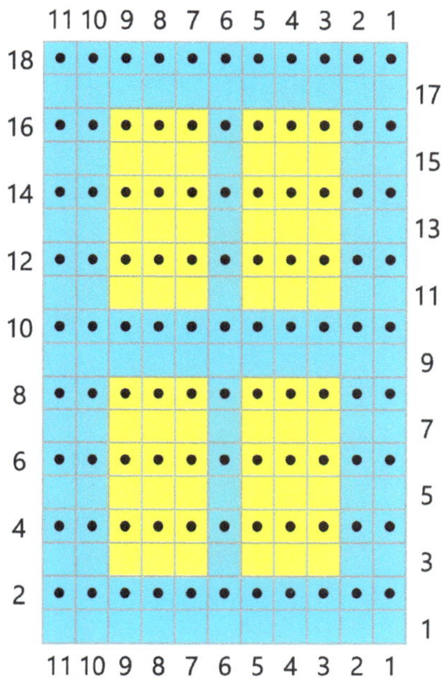

```
      11 10  9  8  7  6  5  4  3  2  1
   18  •  •  •  •  •  •  •  •  •  •  •
   16  •  •        •  •     •  •  •  •  •      17
   14  •  •        •  •     •  •  •  •  •      15
   12                                          13
   10  •  •                                    11
    8  •  •        •  •     •  •  •  •  •       9
    6  •  •        •  •     •  •  •  •  •       7
    4  •  •        •  •     •  •  •  •  •       5
    2  •  •        •  •     •  •  •  •  •       3
                                               1
      11 10  9  8  7  6  5  4  3  2  1
```

Chart Symbols

☐	RS: Knit
•	WS: Knit
🟦	Frame Window color (FW)
🟨	Pane Window color (PW)

Door-11

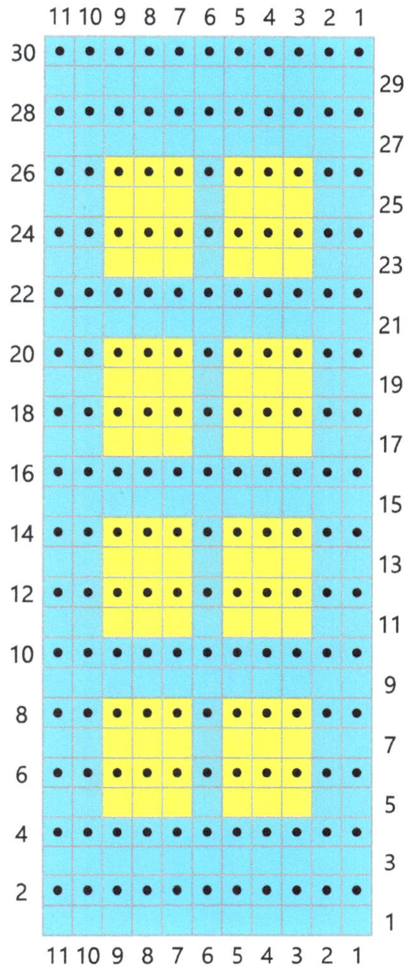

```
      11 10  9  8  7  6  5  4  3  2  1
   30  •  •  •  •  •  •  •  •  •  •  •
   28  •  •  •  •  •  •  •  •  •  •  •    29
   26  •  •        •  •     •  •  •  •  •  27
   24  •  •        •  •     •  •  •  •  •  25
   22                                      23
   20  •  •        •  •     •  •  •  •  •  21
   18  •  •        •  •     •  •  •  •  •  19
   16                                      17
   14  •  •        •  •     •  •  •  •  •  15
   12  •  •        •  •     •  •  •  •  •  13
   10                                      11
    8  •  •        •  •     •  •  •  •  •   9
    6  •  •        •  •     •  •  •  •  •   7
    4  •  •        •  •     •  •  •  •  •   5
    2  •  •  •  •  •  •  •  •  •  •  •      3
                                           1
      11 10  9  8  7  6  5  4  3  2  1
```

Chart Symbols

☐	RS: Knit
•	WS: Knit
🟦	Frame Door color (FD)
🟨	Pane Door color (PD)

Folding Rectangle

Row 2: Knit.

Row 3. Knit to 2 sts bef m, ssk, k2tog; k1, ssk, k2tog, knit to end – 4 sts dec'd; 31-3-31 (47-3-47)

Row 4: Knit.

Row 5: Knit to 2 sts bef m, ssk, cdd, k2tog, knit to end – 4 sts dec'd; 30-1-30 (46-1-46)

Row 6: Knit to 2 sts bef m, ssk, rm. Turn needles with tips parallel and RS's together. With 3rd larger needle, 3-needle BO all sts. Cut yarn and fasten off.

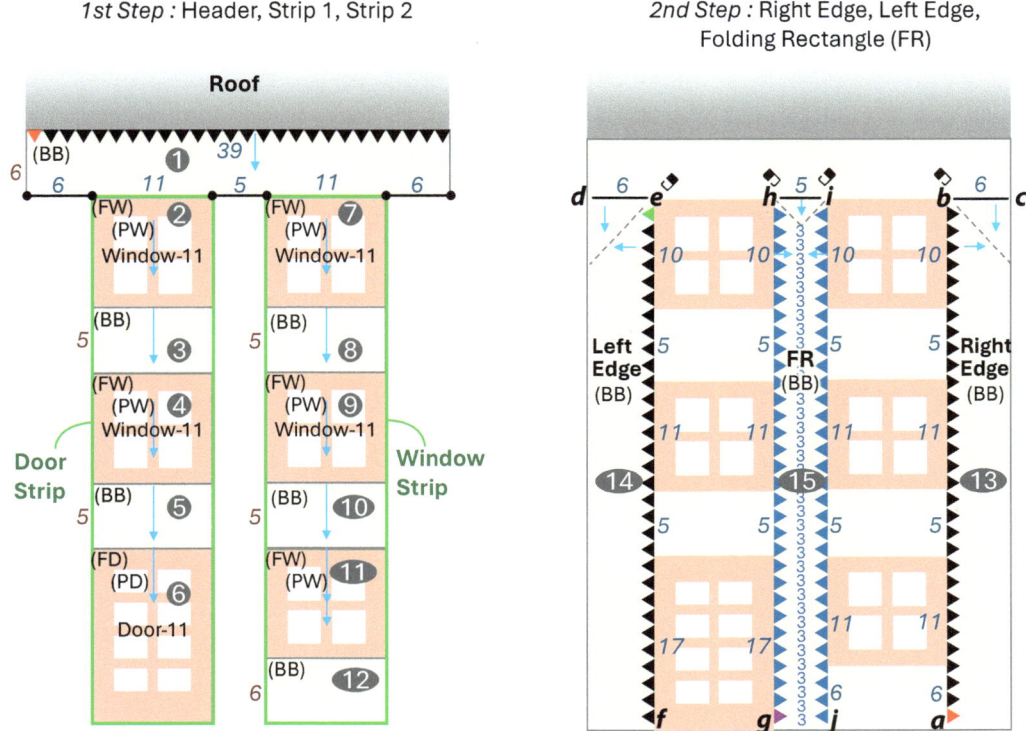

1st Step : Header, Strip 1, Strip 2

2nd Step : Right Edge, Left Edge, Folding Rectangle (FR)

Figure 16: Building 39, 3S Construction

This page has been intentionally left blank.

MISCELLANEOUS BLOCKS AND EMBELLISHMENTS

Miscellaneous Blocks

   Lollipop Tree

   Ice Cream Bar Tree

   Budding Tree

   Carport

   Lamppost

   Garden

Embellishments (made separately and sewn on)

   Cloud

   Sun

   Person

LOLLIPOP TREE BLOCK

- See Figure 17.
- The Lollipop Tree Block is 26 sts wide. The Block is worked first. The Tree Top and Dots are worked separately and sewn on.

Block, Part 1 (Trunk Area)

With color for Sky (SC), CO 24 sts.
Knit 23 rows (on RS 12 ridges including CO). Drop SC but do not cut.
With color for Trunk, knit 4 rows, then cut yarn. Drape SC slightly loosely along right edge, then with SC, knit 24 more rows (26 ridges completed). BO loosely.

Block Part 2 (Sky Area)

Orient completed Trunk Area as shown. With SC, starting at the red triangle, pu&k 26 sts (1 st per garter st ridge) to end of edge.

Knit 83 rows (42 ridges completed including pu&k). BO (on RS) loosely. Set Block aside.

Tree Top

In color for Tree Top, work [Circle].

In color(s) for Dots, with US 0/2 mm needles, work [Dot] 6 times (for 6 Dots).

Turn Dots RS-up. On RS of Tree Top, position Dots as desired on Tree Top and pin from back of Block. Using long yarn tail from Dot, sew to Tree Top. See tutorial "Embellishments" on page 36.

.

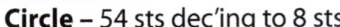

Circle – 54 sts dec'ing to 8 sts

With TC, CO 54 sts.
Rows 2-6: Knit (5 rows).
Row 7 (RS): *K2tog, k1; rep from * to end – 18 sts dec'd; 36 sts.
Rows 8-12: Knit (5 rows). (6 ridges completed)
Row 13 (RS): *K2tog; rep from * to end – 18 sts dec'd; 18 sts.
Rows 14-18: Knit (5 rows). (9 ridges completed)
Row 19 (RS): *K2tog; rep from * to end – 9 sts dec'd; 9 sts.
Cut yarn leaving 20"/50 cm tail. Thread tail onto tapestry needle and insert through rem 9 sts on needle. Pull to close hole, then using mattress st, sew open seam.

Small (Large) Dot – 10 (14) sts dec'ing to 0 sts

With color for Dot, CO 10 (14) sts
(Large only) Row 2 (WS): Knit.
Dec Row: *K2tog, rep from * to end – 5 (7) sts dec'd; 5 (7) sts.
Cut yarn leaving 10"/25 cm tail. Thread tail onto tapestry needle and insert through rem 7 sts on needle, twice. Pull to close hole, take a stitch through 1st and last CO sts.

Join Tree Top to Block

Position Tree Top on Block as shown, aligning bottom of Tree Top anywhere between **a** and **b,** and centering the Tree Top bet the right and left edges of the Block. Pin in several locations from back of Block. Thread tapestry needle with long tail from Tree Top, and sew down edges of Tree Top to Block. See tutorial "Embellishments" on page 36.

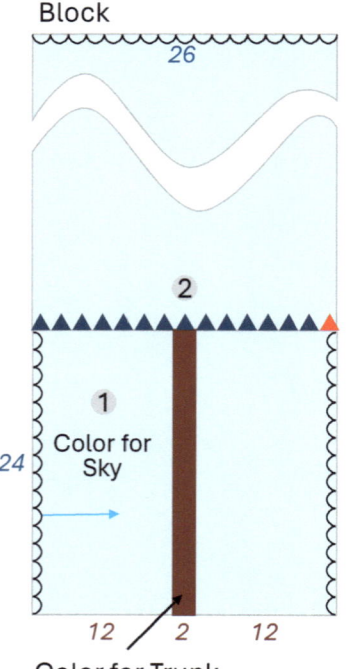

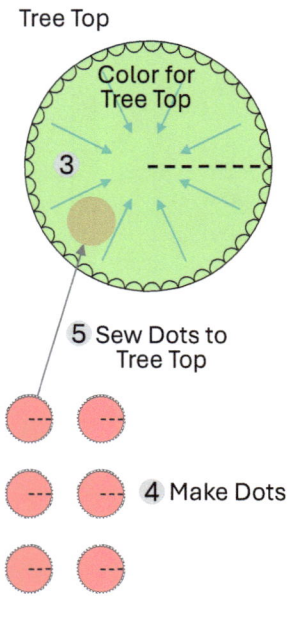

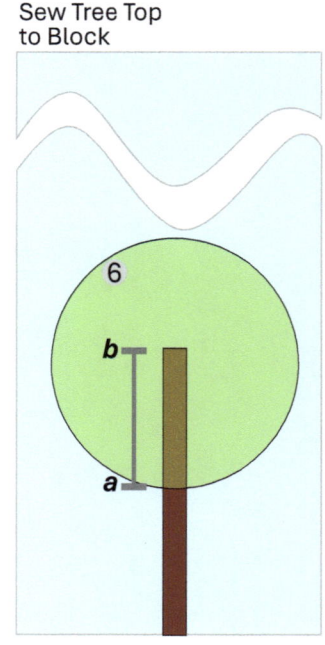

Figure 17:   Lollipop Tree Construction   TOC

Ice Cream Bar Tree

Notes

- This Block is worked in pieces: the Block Background, and then, separately, the Tree Top. The Tree Top is sewn to the Block Background.

- The Tree Top is worked from the Ice Cream Bar Chart. There are no written instructions.

- Increase and decrease rows are RS rows. Increase rows have a kf&b that is worked in the first and last sts of the row and decrease rows start with a k2tog and end with a ssk.

- All WS rows are knit. Bobble locations are marked in pink on the chart. Written instructions for a Bobble are in the pattern stitch box at the bottom of this page.

Chart Symbols

- RS: Knit
- WS: Knit
- RS: Kf&b
- RS: K2tog
- RS: Ssk
- no stitch
- WS: Ssk
- WS: K2tog
- WS: Kf&b
- Cast on
- Bobble
- WS: Slip purlwise with yarn in front

Block Background

Work these parts of the Lollipop Tree on page 24:

- Block, Part 1 (Trunk Area),
- Block, Part 2 (Sky Area).

After completing Row 83, pass right stitch over left st, and fasten off, leaving long tail of 25"/60 cm.

Tree Top

In yarn color for Tree Top and yarn color for Bobble, from Figure 2, work [Ice Cream Bar Tree chart]. After completing Row 83, pass right stitch over left st, and fasten off, leaving tail of 25"/60 cm.

The chart shows the locations of bobbles (pink squares) which are worked on an odd-numbered (RS) row. For example, the first bobble is worked over Rows 7 and 8 as follows:

Row 7: Kf&b, k2 (to pink st), drop TT to back of work, in color for Bobble (BC), work [bobble]. With TT, knit to last st, kf&b – 2 sts inc'd; 12 sts.

Row 8: Cont with TT, knit to bobble, yfwd, sl1 purlwise, ybck, knit to end.

After completing Bobble, drop but do not cut BC. When working the next Bobble, drape it loosely from the prev bobble to the current bobble.

Join Tree Top to Block

Position Tree Top with bottom aligned at location *a* on Figure 17, centering Tree Top bet right and left edges of the Block. Pin Tree Top to Block in place from back of Block. Thread tapestry needle with color for Tree Top, and sew down edges of Tree Top to Block. See tutorial "Embellishments" on page 36.

Bobble

Row 1 (RS): K1, yo, k1, yo, k1 in same st - 4 sts inc'd; 5 sts.
Rows 2-4. Knit.
Row 5 (RS): Slip first 4 sts, 1-by-1, purlwise, to R needle. Knit 5th st, pass 4 slipped sts, 1-by-1, over knitted stitch. Pull yarn to tighten. Drop BC to back of work. Do not cut BC.

TOC

BUDDING TREE

Step 1: Trunk - see Figure 18, Step 1

With SC, CO 50 sts. Knit 11 rows (6 ridges). Drop SC but do not cut. With Trunk Color (TC), knit 2 rows (1 ridge). Cut TC leaving a 30"/75 cm tail, wind up and secure to edge.

Drape SC still attached, drape along edge then knit 6 more rows (6 ridge). BO loosely leaving last st on needle. Do not cut yarn.

Step 2: Sky - see Figure 18, Step 2

With SC still attached, and starting at the red triangle in Figure 18, Step 2, pu&k 12 sts, skipping the first ridge then pu&k 1 st per garter st ridge to corner. Knit 31 rows (16 ridges). Pl 13 sts on holder. Cut yarn leaving long tail for sewing Blocks.

Step 3: Branches - see Figure 18, Step 3

Thread TC (still attached), onto tapestry needle, and with a single strand, starting at the bottom of the Branch numbered 1 in Figure 18 Step 3, and using "stem stitch." Figure 19 shows how to work Stem Stitch), work the first

Branch, then work Branches 2, 3, and 4 in that order.

Note: Stitches should be made in between ridges (in the valleys) if possible. Stitches are 1 ridge/st apart.

The thin dotted lines in Figure 18, Step 3, indicate that yarn is to "travel" from the end of a Branch to the start of the next Branch. To "travel," working on the WS, insert needle through surface bumps of garter stitch ridges.

Tie off on WS when yarn is 6"/15 cm long, and cut a new a new yarn to continue.

Step 4: Stem - see Figure 18, Step 4

With color for Stems, and using chain stitch embroidery, make Stems numbered 1-17 depicted in Step 4 of Figure 18. Work stems in increasing number order, and travel on the WS between the end of one stem and the start of the next. All Stems are worked in a single color but for clarity, are shown in different colors in Figure 18, Step 4.

Step 5: Flowers - see Figure 18, Step 5

With color for Flowers, work French knots in locations indicated in Step 5 of Figure 18. "Travel" the yarn on the

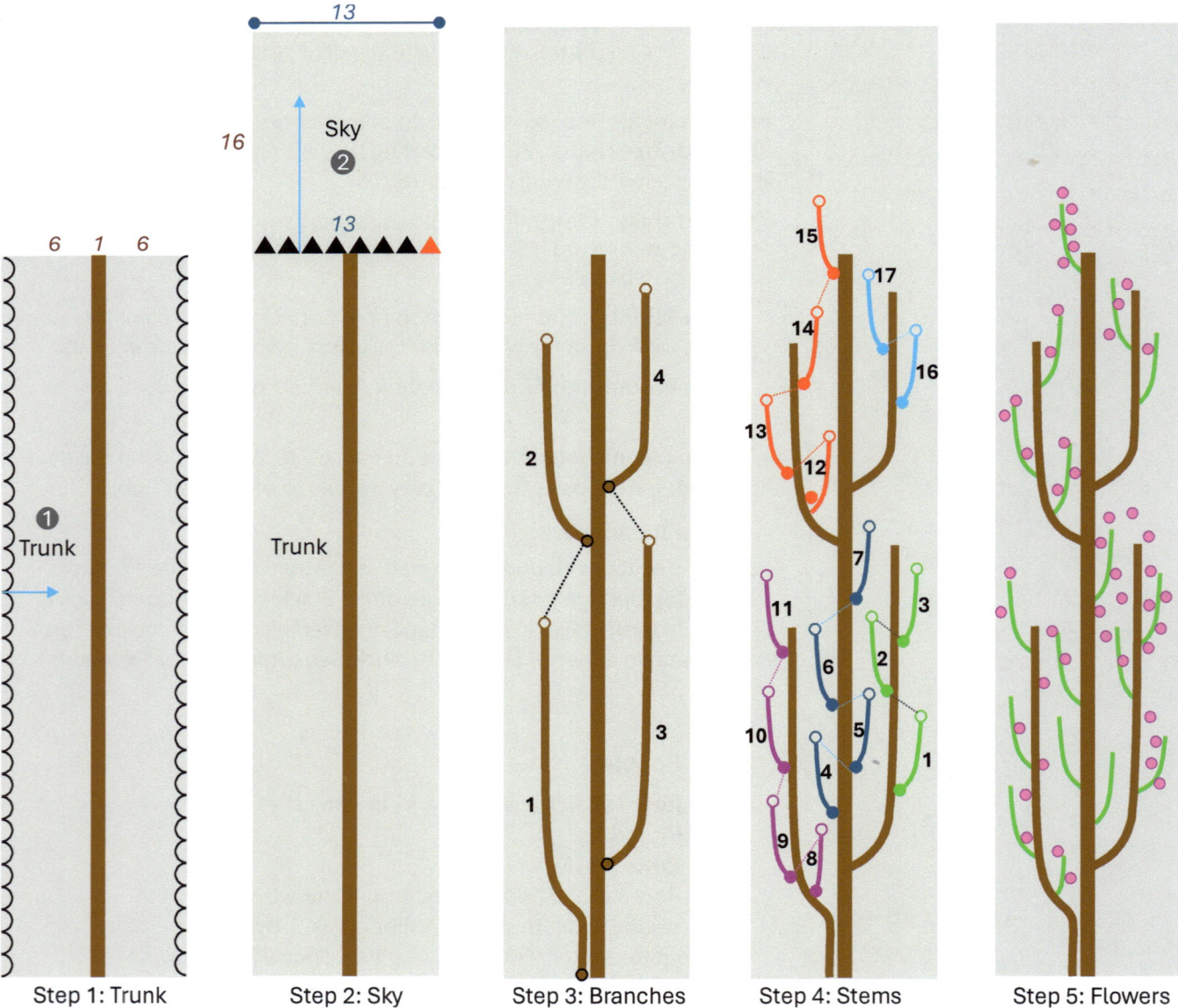

Figure 18: **Budding Tree Construction**

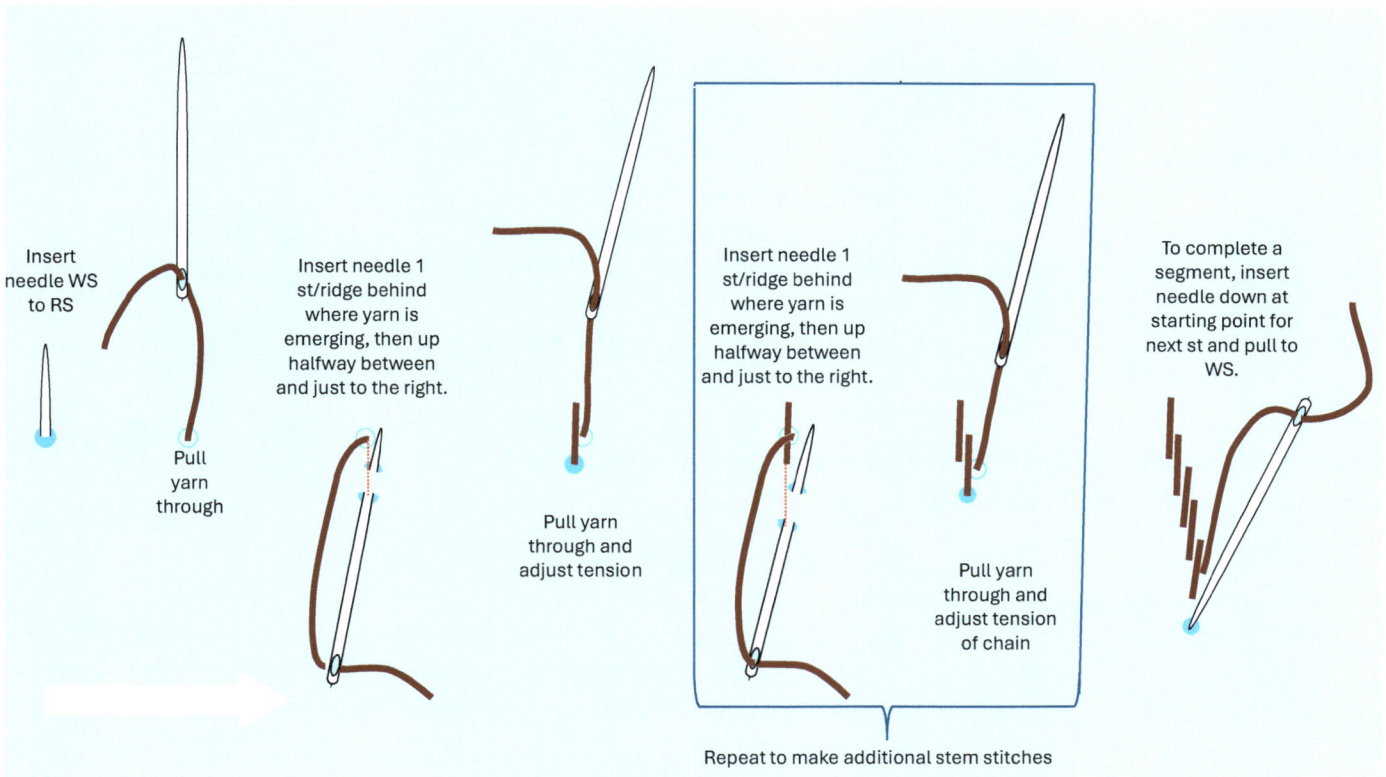

Figure 19: How to Work Stem Stitch Embroidery

WS between Flowers, cutting yarn and tying off when yarn is 6"/15 cm long, and rethreading. Figure 36 on page 35 shows how to work French Knots.

Finishing

On WS, with tapestry needle, weave in ends along WS Branches and stems of the same color. Weave in Flower color yarns along the traveling stitches for Flower on the WS of the work.

CARPORT

For color abbreviations see Figure 20. This block is made in 5 steps.

Step 1: Tires

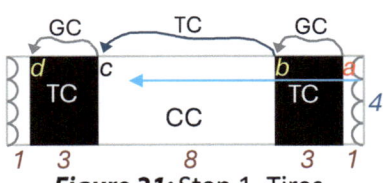

Figure 21: Step 1, Tires

With CC, CO 4 sts.
Knit 1 row. Drop CC but do not cut.
With TC, knit 6 rows (3 ridges). Drop TC but do not cut.

Drape CC slightly loosely from **a** to **b**.
Knit 16 more rows (8 ridges). Drop CC but do not cut.

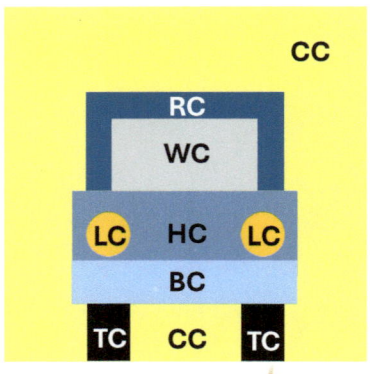

Figure 20: Colors for Carport

Drape TC, slightly loosely, from **b** to **c**. Knit 6 rows (3 ridges). Drop TC and cut.

Drape CC, slightly loosely, from **c** to **d**. Knit 2 rows. BO loosely. Cut yarn.

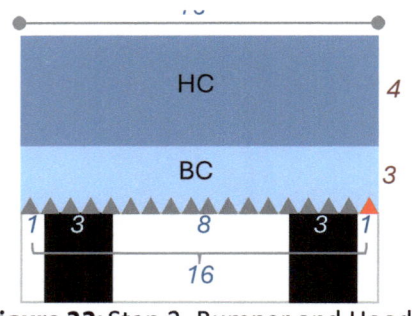

Figure 22: Step 2, Bumper and Hood

Step 2: Bumper and Hood

With BC, and starting at the red triangle in Figure 22, pu&k 16 sts (1 per garter st ridge) to end of edge, while simultaneously tacking draped yarns by alternately inserting needle above and below the draped yarn. "Tacking Draped Yarn" on page 56.

Knit 5 rows. Cut BC.

Continuing with HC, knit 10 rows. Cut HC, and place rem 16 sts on holder or scrap yarn. Set this piece aside.

Step 3: Roof and Window

With CC, CO 32 sts. Pms after 8th and 24th sts.

Row 2 (WS): Knit. Cut CC.
Row 3 (RS): With RC, *Knit to 2 sts bef next m, ssk, k2tog; rep from * once; knit to end – 4 sts dec'd; 28 sts.
Row 4: Knit.
Rows 5 & 6: Rep [Rows 3 & 4] once – 4 sts dec'd; 24 sts. Cut RC.
Rows 7-14: With WC, rep [Rows 3 & 4] 4 times – 16 sts dec'd; 8 sts.
Row 15 (RS): Rep [Row 3] - 4 sts dec'd; 4 sts.
Row 16 (WS): Sl 2 sts knit-wise to R needle, k2tog, psso -- 3 sts dec'd; 1 st. Cut yarn and fasten off.

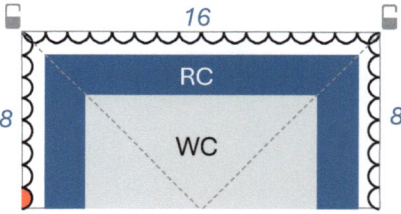

Figure 23: Step 3, Roof and Window

Step 4: Joining top and bottom together

With HC, and starting at red triangle at the bottom-left corner of the top piece of the Car, pu&k 16 sts to end of edge. Knit 1 row.

Turn the bottom piece of the Car so that RS is up. Using a separate needle, insert needle right-to-left, to transfer sts from holder to needle. Turn top and bottom Car pieces so that RS are together and WS are facing out. With HC still attached to top piece, and using the larger 3rd needle, 3-needle BO all sts loosely. Cut HC and fasten off.

Note: the green arrow shows the direction of the 3-needle BO.

Figure 24: Joining top and bottom pieces of Car

Step 5: Border

Use (4) US 4/3.5 mm dpns.

On RS, starting at the red triangle, with CC and a dpn, pu&k 21 sts to next corner. Onto 2nd dpn, pu&k 16 sts (1 per CO st) on top edge, and onto 3rd dpn, pu&k 21 sts on left edge – 58 sts.

Row 2: Knit.

Row 3: Knit to last st on needle, kf&b in last st of needle and 1st st of next needle; rep from * once, knit to end – 4 sts inc'd; 62 sts (22-18-22).

Row 4: Knit.

Rows 5-10: Rep [Rows 3 & 4] 3 more times – 12 sts inc'd; 74 sts. Do not rm m's. BO loosely, placing m's on edge at top-right and top-left corners.

Headlights - make 2

With LC, CO 10.

Row 1 (WS): K2tog 5 times – 5 sts dec'd; 5 sts.

Cut yarn leaving 10"/25 cm tail. Thread tail onto tapestry needle and sew headlight to Hood at location shown in Figure 20.

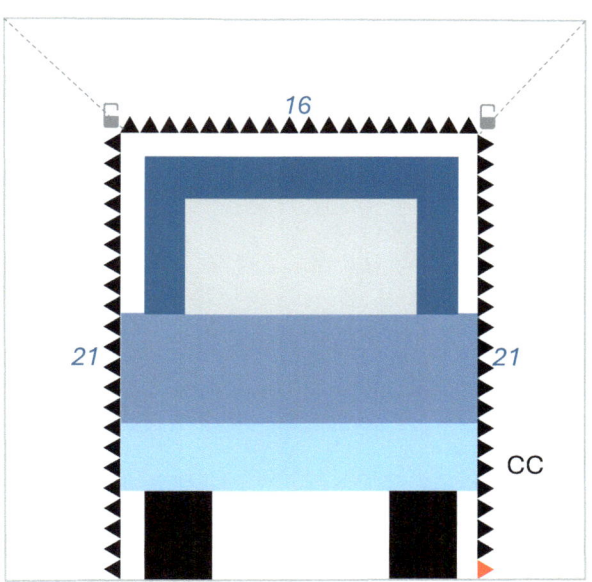

Figure 25: Border

The Carport is now complete. Work the Roof type (Sloped, Truncated, or Shallow Peaked) indicated in Figure 2. If Roof is worked from bottom up, generate 26 sts by pu&k between m's. Otherwise, work Roof separately and sew to Carport.

LAMPPOST BLOCK

The Lamppost Block is a 13 st wide block worked in 4 steps: Pole, Sky, Base, and Lamp, as shown in Figure 27.

Step 1: Pole

With Sky color (SC) for Strip, CO 28 sts.
Knit 11 rows (6 ridges including CO row).
Drop SC but do not cut.
With W, knit 2 rows. Cut W.
With SC, knit 12 rows. BO loosely. Do not cut yarn.

Step 2: Sky

Starting at red triangle, with SC, pu&k 13 sts (1 st per garter st ridge) to end of edge. Knit 75 rows (38 ridges). BO loosely.

Step 3: Base

With W, and starting at the red triangle in the second from left illustration, pu&k 7 sts on short edge of Pole piece, starting at the 4th ridge from the right, and generating 1 st per garter stitch ridge, making the 7th pu&k in the 4th ridge from the opposite edge.

Work [Base].

Base - 7 sts dec'ing to 0 sts

Rows 2-4: Knit.
Row 5: K2tog, knit to last 2 sts ssk – 2 sts dec'd; 5 sts.
Rows 6-8: Knit.
Rows 7-10: Rep [Rows 5-8] once more – 2 sts dec'd; 3 sts.
Row 11: Cdd – 2 sts dec'd; 1 st.
Cut yarn and fasten off, leaving 8"/20 cm tail.

Fold Base toward RS of Block, matching the two letter *a*'s in Figure 27.

Thread tail onto tapestry needle and tack to the center ridge, 5th stitch in from edge, taking several stitches to attach. The side edges are left open. Fasten off. Weave in tail on WS on sts worked in W.

Step 4: Lamp

Turn Block to RS and orient so Sky area is at the top. With color for light (LC), and starting at the red triangle (at Ridge 1 and Stitch 6 of the Sky piece), pu&k 3 stitches in the frowny faces (1 pu&k per stitch, to Stitch 8. Work [Light].

Thread yarn tail onto tapestry needle, and sew to Sky at location shown in Figure 27. See "Embellishments" on page 36.

Light - 3 sts inc'ing to 7 sts, dec'ing to 3 sts

Rows 2-4: Knit.
Row 5: Kf&b, k1, kf&b – 2 sts inc'd; 5 sts.
Row 6: Knit.
Row 7: Kf&b, k3, kf&b – 2 sts inc'd; 7 sts.
Row 8: Knit.
Row 9: Kf&b, k5, kf&b – 2 sts inc'd; 9 sts.
Row 10: Knit.
Drop LC.
With W,
Rows 11: K2tog, k5, ssk – 2 sts dec'd 7 sts.
Row 12: Knit.
Row 13: K2tog, k3, ssk – 2 sts dec'd; 5 sts.
Row 14: Knit.
Row 15: K2tog, k1, ssk – 2 sts dec'd; 3 sts.
Row 16: Knit.
BO loosely.
Cut yarn and fasten off, leaving 8"/20 cm tail.

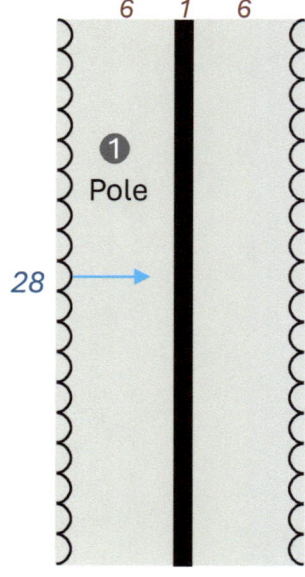

Step 1: Pole

Figure 26: Step 1

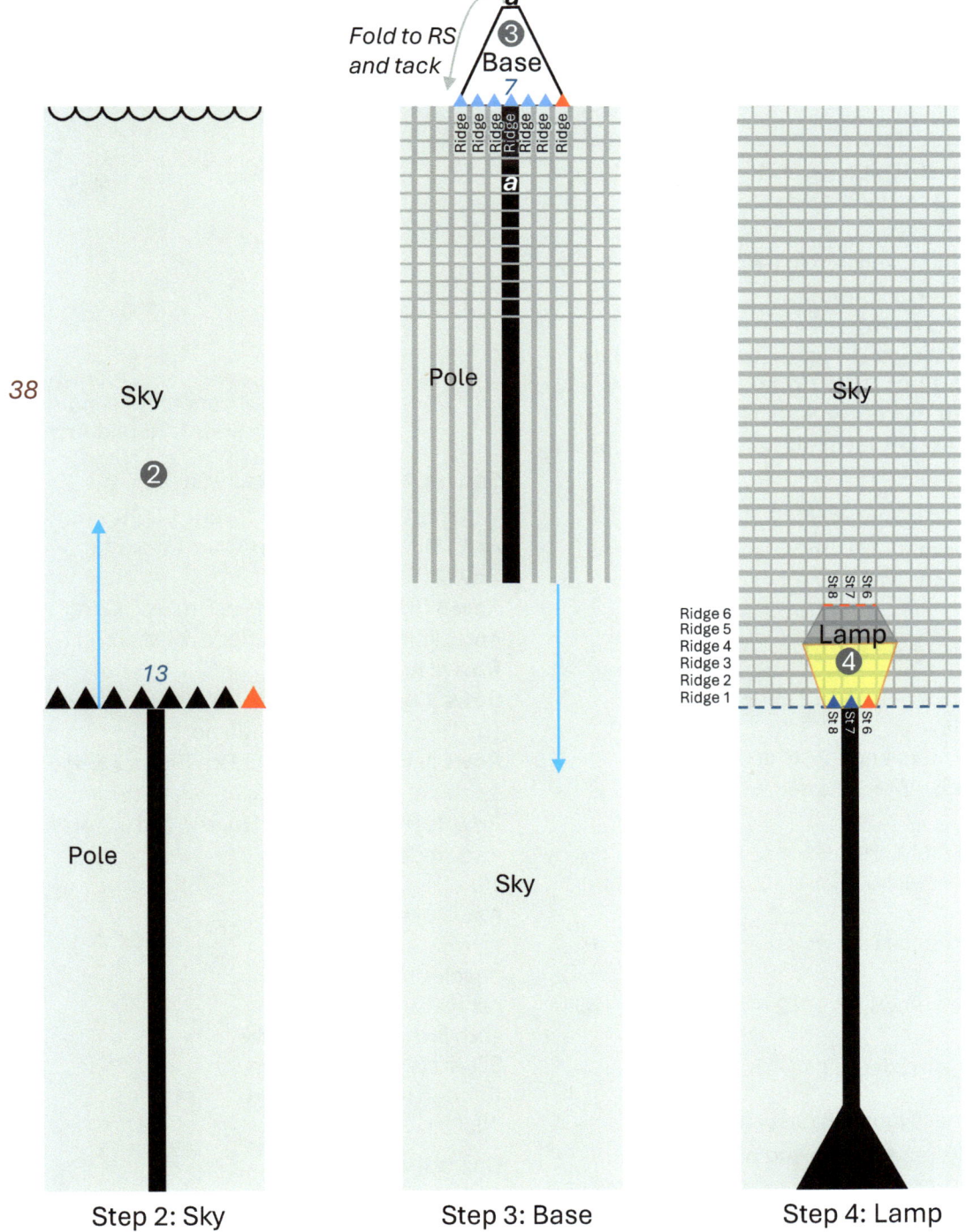

Step 2: Sky

Step 3: Base

Step 4: Lamp

Figure 27: Steps 2-4

Garden Block

- The Block is knitted, then vines and flowers are embroidered on.
- For the Arch, work either the **Round Arch** (this page) or **Square Arch**.
- Construction order is: Arch, Corners (for Round Arch only), Left Fence, Right Fence, Sky.
- Fence Color (FC) is the color used for the vertical fence slats and the Arch.

Round Arch - see (Step 1a)

With FC, CO 15, pm (a), CO 27, pm (c), CO 15 – 57 sts (15-27-15)

Rows 2-4: Knit 3 rows.

Cut FC.

Rows 5 & 6: With SC, Knit.

Row 7: Cont with SC, knit to m, *k2tog, k1; rep to next m, sm, knit to end – 9 sts dec'd; 48 sts (15-18-15).

Rows 8-12: Knit 5 rows.

Row 13: Knit to m, *k2tog; rep to next m, sm, knit to end – 9 sts dec'd; 39 sts (15-9-15).

Rows 14-18: Knit 5 rows.

Row 19: Knit to 1st m, cdd 3 times (to next m), knit to end – 6 sts dec'd; 33 sts (15-3-15). Mv ma and mb to edge bet 15th and 16th sts from ends. Pm (b) at top of arch.

Row 20: Knit to 1 st bef 1st m, sl2 knitwise, k2tog, p2sso, turn RS tog, and 3-needle BO all sts.

Corner 1(Cr1) - see Figure 28 (Step 1b)

In the space labeled "Cr1," with SC, and starting at red triangle, pu&k 14 sts (1 per CO st bet **a** and **b**. Work [Corner].

Corner- 14 sts dec'ing to 1 st

Row 2 (WS): K2tog, k4, w&t – 1 st dec'd; 13 sts.

Row 3 (RS): Knit.

Row 4: K3tog, knit to end – 2 sts dec'd; 11 sts.

Row 5: K3tog, k2, w&t – 2 sts dec'd; 9 sts.

Row 6: Knit.

Row 7: K2tog, knit to last 2 sts, ssk – 2 sts dec'd; 7 sts.

Row 8: Knit to center st, kf&b, knit to end – 1 st inc'd; 8 sts.

Row 9: K2tog, knit to last 2 sts, ssk – 2 sts dec'd; 6 sts.

Row 10: Knit.

Rows 11-14: Rep [Rows 9 & 10] 2 times – 4 sts dec'd; 2 sts.

Row 15: K2tog – 1 st dec'd; 1 st.

Corner 2 (Cr2) - see Figure 28 (Step 1b)

Drape SC, slightly loosely, from end of Cr1 to green triangle at **b**. Starting at green triangle, pu&k 14 sts bet **b** and **c** (1 per CO st). Work [Corner]. Cut yarn and fasten off.

Continue at *Left Fence*, page 33.

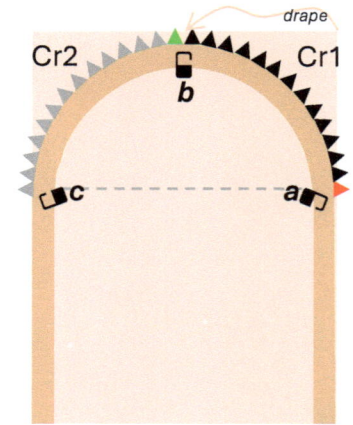

Step 1a: Round Arch 2

Step 1b: Corners for Round Arch
Figure 28: Step 1 (Round Arch)

Square Arch - see Figure 29 (Step 1)

With FC, CO 28, pm, CO 19, pm, CO 28, pm – 75 sts. *Note:* M's placed during CO are magenta.

Row 2 (WS): Knit.

Row 3 (RS): *Knit to 2 sts bef, m, ssk, k2tog; rep from * once, knit to end – 4 sts dec'd; 71 sts (27-17-27).

Row 4: Knit.

Rows 5 & 6: Rep [Rows 3 & 4] once – 4 sts dec'd; 67 sts (26-15-26). Drop FC, but do not cut.

Rows 7-18: Cont with SC. Rep [Rows 3 & 4] 6 times -- 24 sts dec'd; 43 sts (20-3-20).

Row 19: Knit to 2 sts bef m, ssk, cdd, k2tog, knit to end – 4 sts dec'd; 39 sts (19-1-19).

Row 20: Knit to 1 st bef m, rm's, k2tog. Rotate needles so tips are parallel and RS are tog. With 3rd needle, 3-needle BO all sts. Cut yarn, insert through rem loop, fasten off.

On L edge of Square Arch, pm (c) on the 15th CO st from bottom. Pm (a) on R edge, on 15th CO st from bottom.

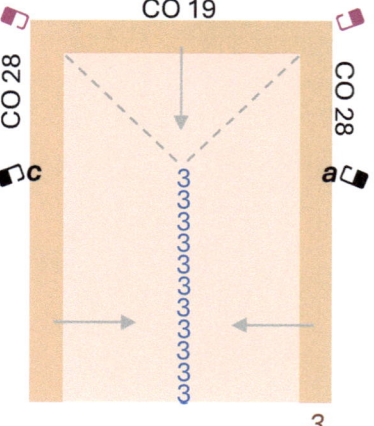

Step 1: Square Arch 3
Figure 29: Step 1 (Square Arch)

Left Fence - see Figure 30 (Step 2)

Note: When working Fences, do not cut SC and FC until instructed to do so. Drape non-working yarn along R edge bet uses.

With SC, and starting at green triangle at *c*, pu&k 15 sts to bottom-left corner of Arch. Work [Fence]. Cut SC.

Fence - 15 sts

Rows 1-2: With SC, knit 2 rows.

Note: Skip Row 1 during first rep. Drop SC.

Rows 3-6: With FC, knit 4 rows. Drop FC.

Rows 7-18: Rep [Rows 1-6] 2 more times. Drop FC, cut.

Rows 19 & 20: With SC, knit 2 rows. BO loosely.

Right Fence - see Figure 30 (Step 2)

With SC, and starting at red triangle at bottom-right corner of Arch, pu&k 15 sts to *a* (1 st per CO st). Work [Fence].

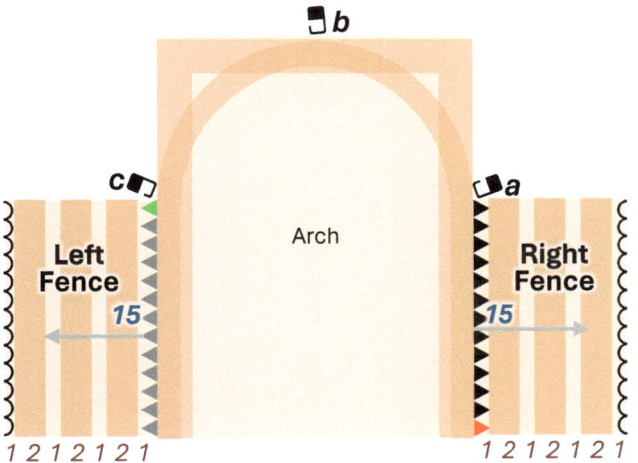

Step 2: Fences (for both Arches)

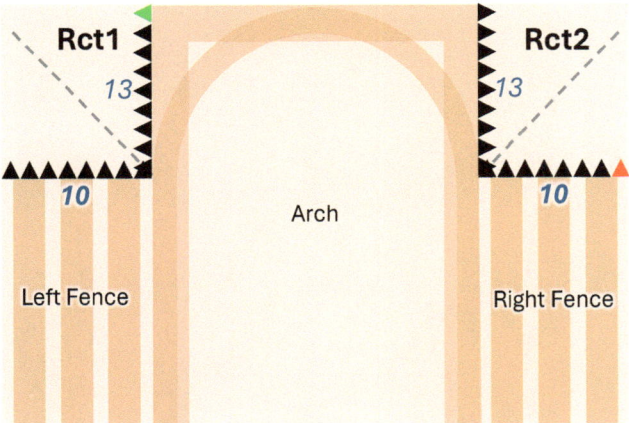

Step 3: Rectangles (for both Arches)

Figure 30: Square Arch (Step 1), Fences (Step 2)

Rct1 - see Figure 30 (Step 3)

With SC, starting at green triangle, pu&k 13 sts to mc, transfer mc to needle, pu&k 10 sts to next corner. Work [Rectangle] – 18 sts dec'd; 5 sts (4-1).

Next row (WS): Rm. BO loosely, working a K2tog at beg of BO. Cut yarn and fasten off.

Rectangle- 23 sts dec'ing to 5 sts

Row 2 (WS): Knit.

Row 3 (RS): Knit to 2 sts bef m, ssk, k2tog, knit to end – 2 sts dec'd; 21 sts.

Row 4: Knit.

Rows 5-18: Rep [Rows 3 & 4] 7 times – 14 sts dec'd; 7 sts.

Row 19 (WS): Rep [Row 3] – 2 sts dec'd; 5 sts.

Rct2 - see Figure 30 (Step 3)

In space "Rct 2," with SC yarn still attached from Right Fence, and starting at red triangle, pu&k 10 sts to ma, transfer ma to needle, pu&k 13 sts to next corner. Work [Rectangle] – 18 sts dec'd; 5 sts (1-4).

Next row (WS): Rm. BO loosely, working a K2tog on the last 2 sts of the BO. Cut yarn and fasten off.

Note: Do not cut SC and FC until instructed to do so. Drape non-working yarn along R edge bet uses.

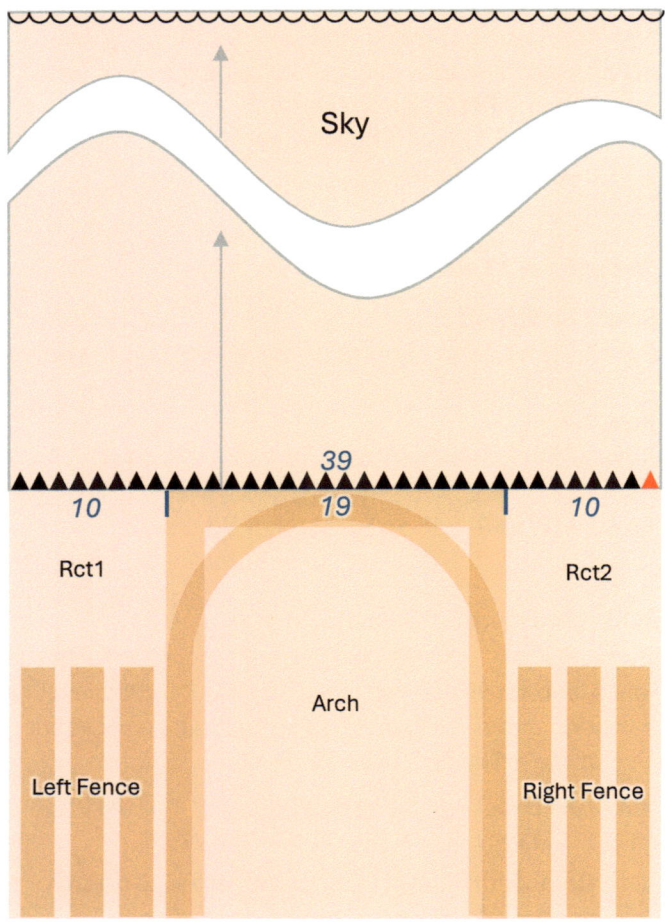

Sky

With SC still attached from Rct2, pu&k 39 sts across the top of piece (10 sts on Rct2, 19 sts on Archway, 10 sts on Rct1).

Knit 79 rows (40 ridges complete). Place sts on holder. Cut SC and fasten off. Weave in all yarn ends before working embroidery embellishments.

Embroidery Tips

- Thread yarn onto a tapestry/finishing needle,
- Work with a single strand of yarn on RS of work,
- To fix mistakes, unthread needle and unpick sts, re-thread.

Figure 32: Sky Construction

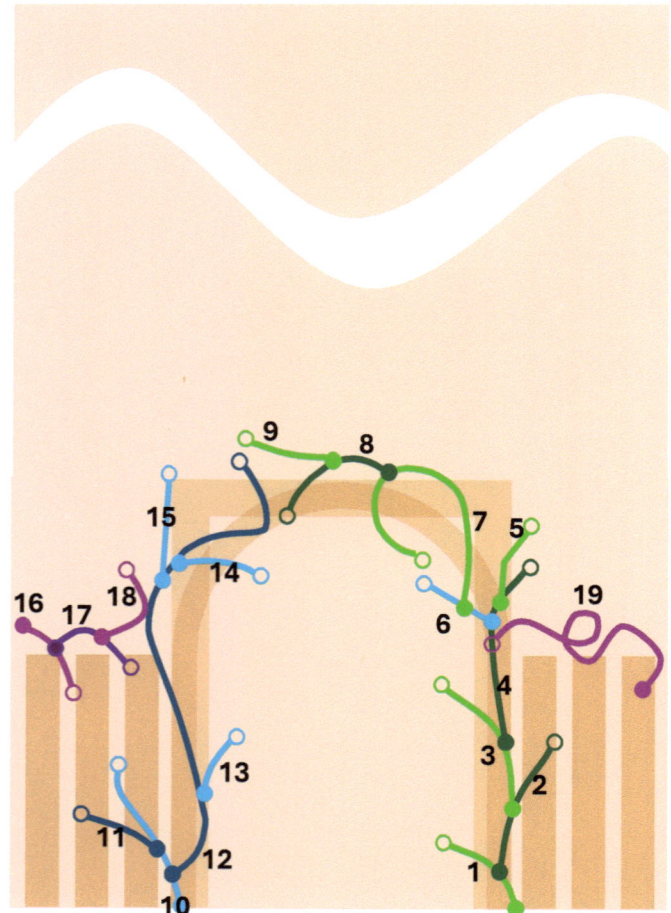

Figure 33: Vine Construction

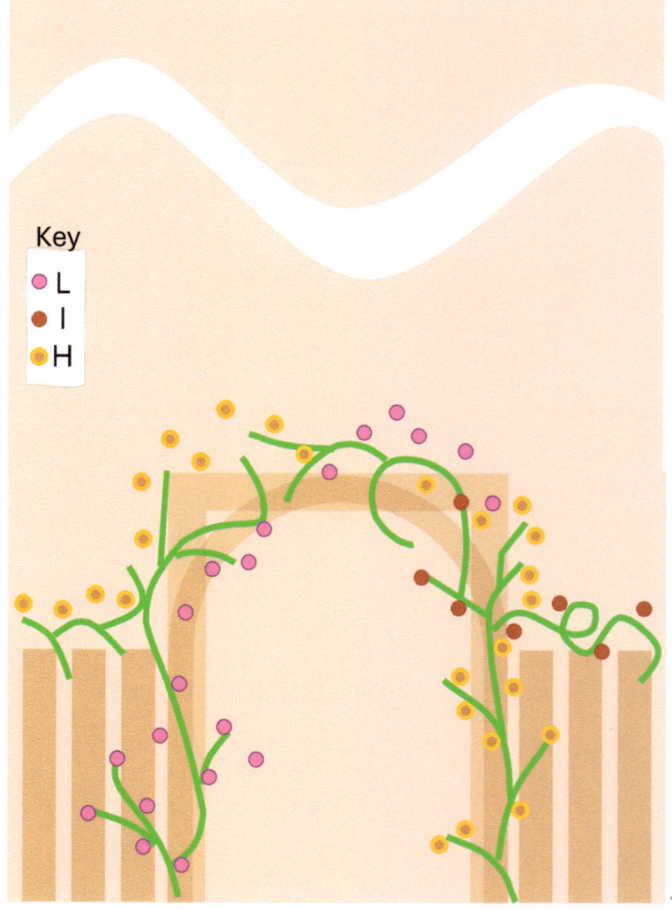

Figure 34: Flowers

Key

L
I
H

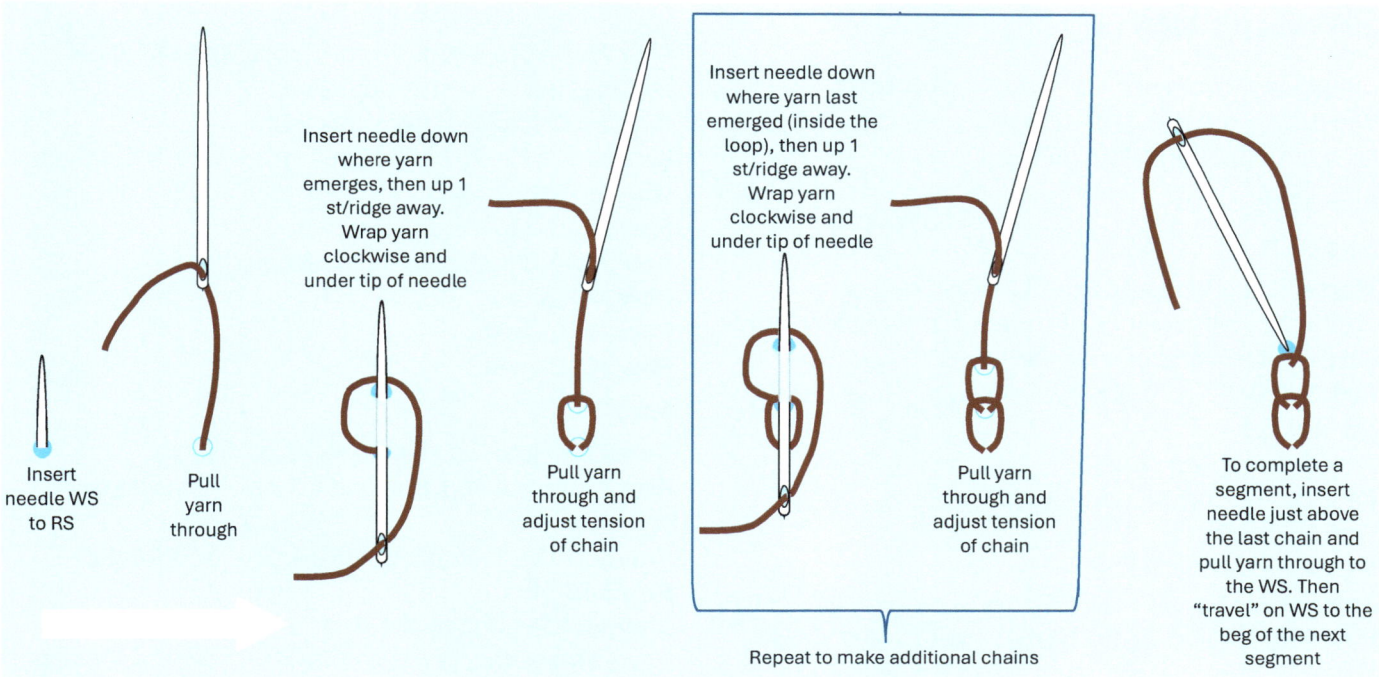

Figure 35: How to do Chain Stitch Embroidery

Vines

Work vines using chain stitch. Stitch length is 1 ridge high or 1 st wide. Figure 33 shows the position and shapes of the vine segments, numbered 1 to 19, and worked in that order. Vines are worked in the color specified in Figure 2 but shown in different colors in Figure 33 for clarity.

The first chain stitch of a segment is made at the solid filled circle of segment (see Figure 33), and last chain stitch of segment is made at unfilled circle. See Figure 35 for how to make chain stitches. Cut a length of yarn no longer than 30"/75 cm so that the friction of repeatedly pulling through doesn't weaken and break the yarn. Work until the yarn is about 6"/15 cm then fasten off on the WS and weave-in the end on the WS sts of the segment.

Don't break yarn between segments. "Travel" back by making 1 st in each WS st of just-completed segment to reach the starting point for next segment.

Do not pull sts too tight. Adjust tension of each st after it is created, pulling up slack yarn so all sts are evenly sized.

Flowers

There are three colors of flowers: L, I, and H, shown in the Key of Figure 34. Cut yarn of length 30"/75 cm or less. Make a French Knot at each dot. To make a French Knot, see instructions in Figure 36. A French Knot ends with the yarn on the WS. Do not cut yarn between French Knots. Travel to next starting point on WS, taking a stitch in a garter st bump to avoid long floats.

TOC

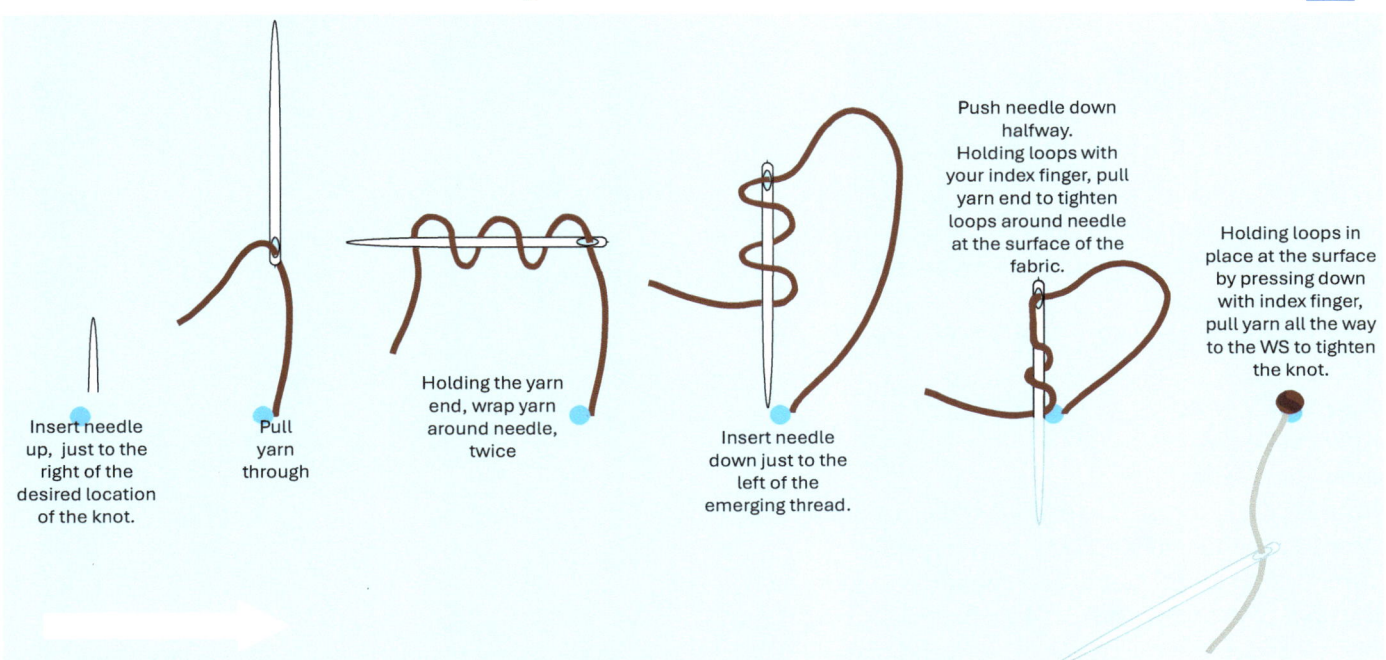

Figure 36: How to Make a French Knot

EMBELLISHMENTS

Cloud - work from written instructions or chart
With US 0/2.5 mm needles, CO 39 sts. Pm's after 11th (m1), 17th (m2), and 30th (m3) sts.

Row 2 (WS): Knit.

Section 1

This section is worked on the 11 sts bet beg of row to 1st m. Stitch counts are for # of sts rem in this section.
Bet beg of row and next marker
Row 3 (RS): K2, (k2tog, k1) 2 times, k2tog, w&t – 3 sts dec'd; 8 sts.
Row 4: Knit to last st, w&t.
Row 5: K2, k2tog, k1, w&t – 1 st dec'd; 7 sts.
Row 6: K3, w&t.
Row 7: K2, w&t.
Row 8: K1, w&t.
Row 9 (RS): K2tog, k2 (to 1st m1), sm – 1 st dec'd; 6 sts.
This section ends at the 1st m. Sm to R needle.

Section 2

This section is worked on the 6 sts bet 1st and 2nd m's. Stitch counts are for the # of sts rem in this section.

Row 9 (continued): K1, k2tog twice, w&t – 2 sts dec'd; 4 sts.
Row 10: K2, w&t.
Row 11: Knit to 2nd m. Sm to R needle.

Section 3

This section is worked on the 13 sts between the 2nd and 3rd m's. Stitch counts are for the # of sts rem in this section.

Row 11 (continued): K1, (k2tog, k1) 3 times, k2tog, w&t – 4 sts dec'd; 9 sts.
Row 12: Knit to 1 st bef m2, w&t.
Row 13: K3, k2tog, k2, w&t – 1 st dec'd; 8 sts.
Row 14: K4, w&t.
Row 15: K2tog, k1, w&t – 1 st dec'd; 7 sts.
Row 16: K1, w&t.
Row 17: Knit to 3rd m. Sm to R needle.

Section 4

This section is worked on the 9 sts between the 3rd m and the end of the row. Stitch counts are for the # of sts rem in this section.
Row 17 (continued): K2, (k2tog, k1) twice, w&t – 2 sts dec'd; 7 sts.
Row 18: K5, w&t.
Row 19: K4, w&t.
Row 20: K3, w&t.
Row 21: K1, k2tog, knit to end – 1 st dec'd; 6 sts.
Row 22: Knit to end (all 23 sts rem on needle).
Turn work to the RS. Count and confirm that there are: 6 sts bet start of row and m1, 4 sts bet m1 and m2, 7 sts bet m2 and m3, and 6 sts bet m3 and end of row. Rm's.

Crescent - worked over rem 23 sts
Row 23: Knit to 8 sts from end, k2tog, knit to 1 st bef end, w&t last st – 1 st dec'd; 22 sts.
Row 24: Knit to 3 sts from end, w&t.
Row 25: K9, k2tog, knit to last 2 sts, w&t – 1 st dec'd; 21 sts.
Row 26: Knit to the last 6 sts, w&t.
Row 27: Knit to the last 3 sts, w&t.
Row 28: K8, w&t.
Row 29: K5, w&t.
Row 30: K2, w&t.

Base

Row 31: Knit to last st, kf&b – 1 st inc'd; 22 sts.
Row 32: Knit to end, turn and CO 2 sts – 2 sts inc'd; 24 sts.
Row 33: Kf&b, knit to end, kf&b – 2 sts inc'd; 26 sts.
Row 34: Knit.
Row 35: Kf&b, knit to last st, kf&b – 2 sts inc'd; 28 sts.
Rows 36-40: Knit. (5 rows)
Row 41: K2tog, knit to last 2 sts, ssk – 2 sts dec'd; 26 sts.
Row 42: Knit.
Rows 43 & 44: Rep [Rows 41 & 42] – 2 sts dec'd; 24 sts.

BO loosely working a k3tog at beg of row and sssk at end of row.

Step 1: Sections 1-4

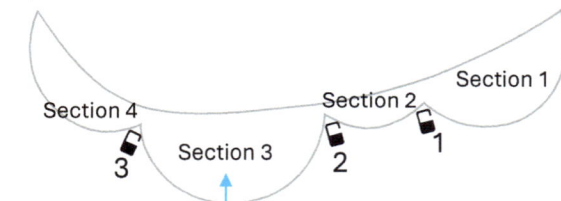

Step 2: Crescent

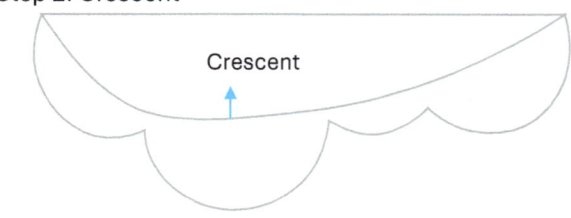

Step 3: Base

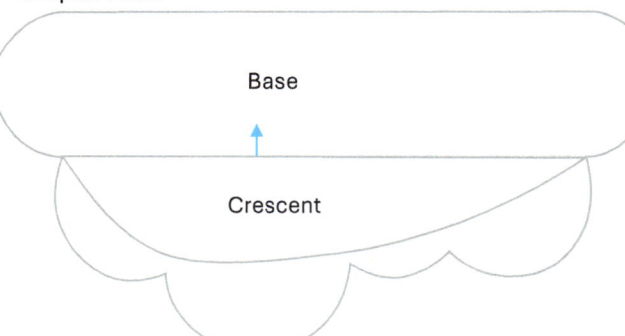

Figure 37: Big Cloud Construction Overview

Cloud

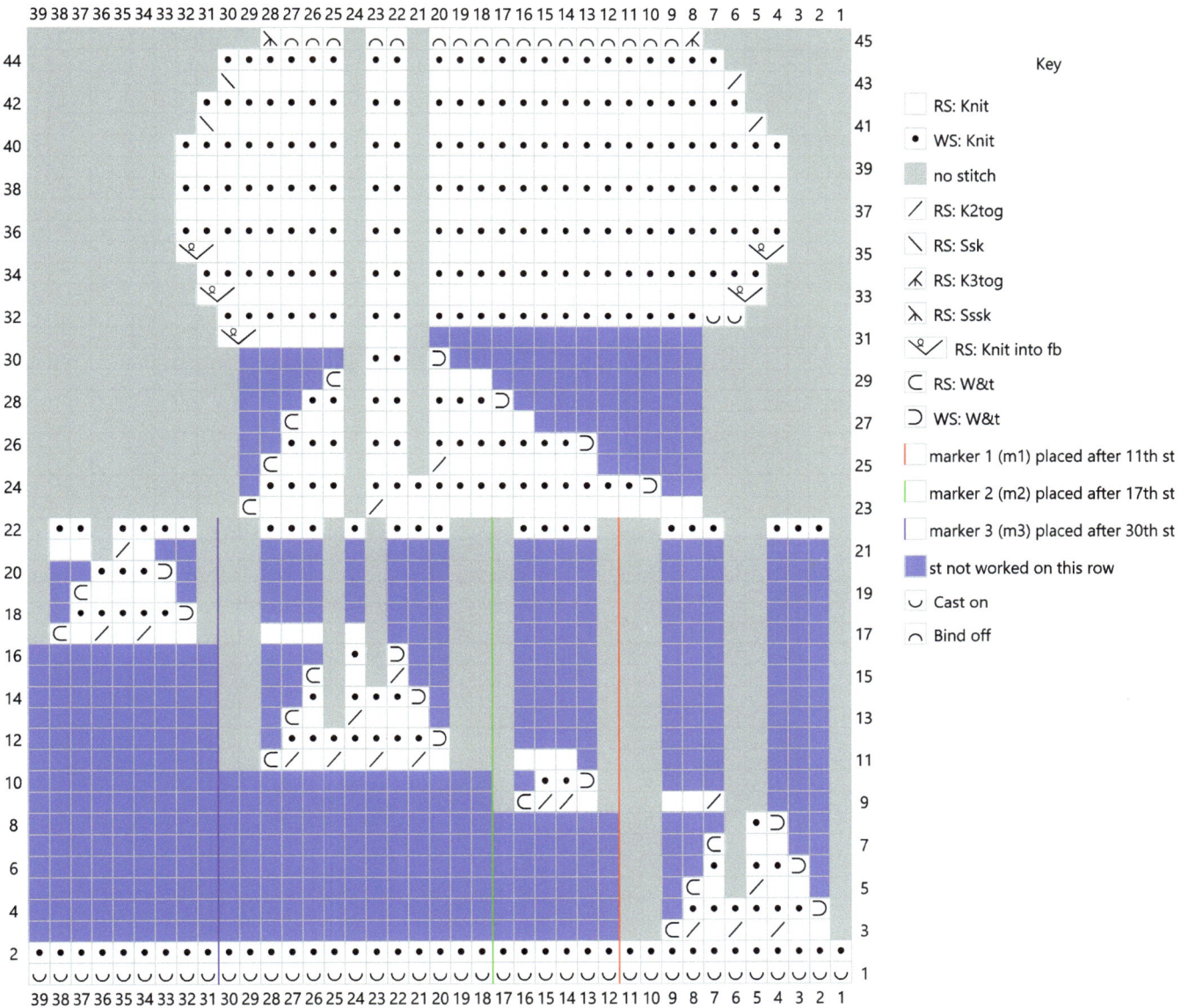

Key

RS: Knit
• WS: Knit
no stitch
╱ RS: K2tog
╲ RS: Ssk
⋏ RS: K3tog
⋋ RS: Sssk
⌄ RS: Knit into fb
⊂ RS: W&t
⊃ WS: W&t
marker 1 (m1) placed after 11th st
marker 2 (m2) placed after 17th st
marker 3 (m3) placed after 30th st
st not worked on this row
⌣ Cast on
⌢ Bind off

TOC

Sun

- See Figure 38 for construction.
- The Sun has 8 Rays that are worked from a single yarn strand.
- Stitches for the Center are pu&k along the inner edge of the completed Rays. The Center is worked flat, then a small seam is sewn.
- The Sun is positioned between Blocks 1.8 and 1.9. See the photo on the 1st page of the pattern for positioning.

Ray 1

With Ray Color (RC), CO 2. Work [Ray].

Ray 2

CO 1 – 1 st inc'd; 2 sts.
Work [Ray].

Rays 3-8

Work as for Ray 2.

Cut yarn and fasten off, leaving 30"/75 cm tail. Wind up tail and secure to edge.

Place completed Sun, RS up, at location shown on Figure 2. Place a safety pin or removable marker in each Ray, pinning from the WS. Working on RS, using long tail from Ray, sew around the edges of all Rays. See "Tacking Embellishments" on page 45 for more information.

Center

Starting at the red triangle, pu&k 32 sts (4 sts per Ray) on the inner edges of the Rays. Work [Center].

Using mattress st and long tail from Center, sew open seam, then fasten off. Tie CO and BO tails of the Rays together.

Ray - 2 sts inc'ing to 10 sts, dec'ing to 1 st

Row 2 (WS): Knit, turn and CO 2 – 2 sts inc'd; 4 sts.
Row 3: (RS): Knit.
Rows 4-7: Rep [Rows 2 & 3] twice – 4 sts inc'd; 8 sts.
Row 8: Rep [Row 2] – 2 sts inc'd; 10 sts.
BO leaving last st on needle.

Center - 32 sts dec'ing to 8 sts

Row 2 and even-numbered (WS) rows to X: Knit.
Row 3: (RS): *K2tog, k2; rep from * to end – 8 sts dec'd; 24 sts.
Row 5: *K2tog, k1, rep from * to end – 8 sts dec'd; 16 sts.
Row 7: *K2tog; rep from * to end – 8 sts dec'd; 8 sts.
Cut yarn leaving 12"/30 cm tail. Thread tail onto tapestry needle. Insert needle through 8 rem sts on needle. Pull to tighten and fasten off securely.

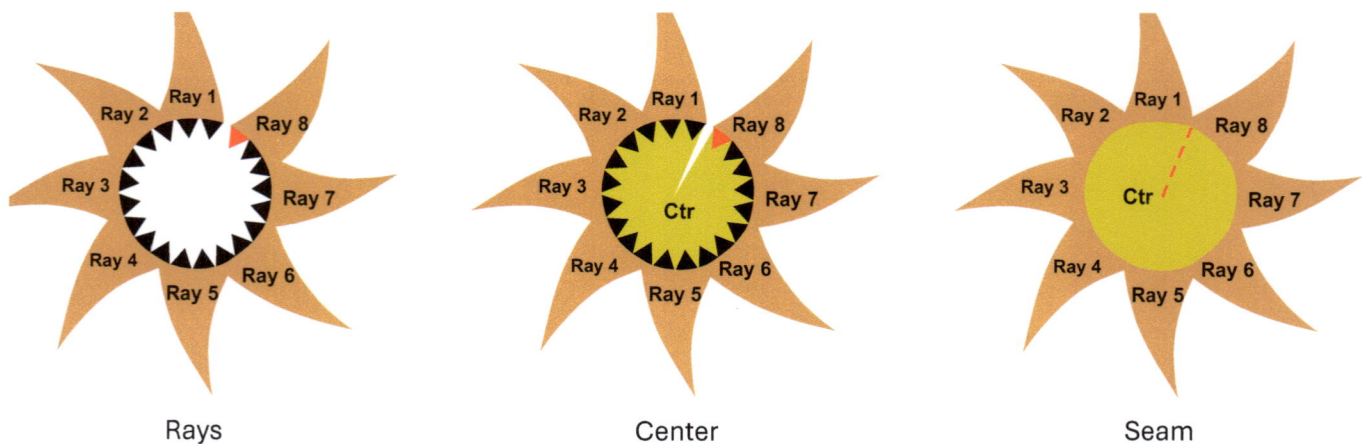

Rays   Center   Seam

Figure 38: Sun Construction

Person

This is a person you can knit and sew onto your blanket if desired. It was not used in the sample.

Leave 10"/25 cm tails when cutting off yarns, used later for tacking the person to the blanket.

Shirt

Left Arm

With color for shirt, CO 7 sts.
BO 4 sts – (2 sts on L needle, unworked; 1 st on R needle, already worked). K1, turn, leaving last st unworked – 3 sts.

Torso

First row: K2, turn and CO 2 sts – 2 sts inc'd; 5 sts.
Knit 2 rows.
Next row: Knit to last 2 sts, w&t.
Knit 2 rows.
BO 2 sts – (2 sts on L needle, unworked; 1 st on R needle, already worked). k1, turn leaving last st unworked – 3 sts.

Right Arm

K2, turn and CO 4 sts – 7 sts.
BO until 2 sts rem on L needle. Ssk, then BO this st. Cut yarn and fasten off.
Tie together CO and BO tails of Torso to draw in neck slightly.

Pants

Left Leg

With color for pants, CO 8 sts, pm. Then onto same needle, starting at bottom-left corner of Shirt, pu&k 2 sts on bottom, in the 1st and 3rd ridges of the Shirt's edge – 10 sts (8-2).

Row 2: Knit.
Row 3: BO 7 sts (until 1 st rem on L needle bef m), rm, k2tog, pm, turn, leaving last st on L needle unworked – 3 sts.

Right Leg

Row 3: K1, turn and CO 6 sts – 9 sts (8-1).
Row 4: Knit to 1 sts bef m, rm, k2tog
Slipping 1st st purlwise, BO all sts.
Cut yarn leaving 12"/30 cm and fasten off.

Head

With color for head, pu&k 1 st at center to top of shirt. Kyok. Knit 4 rows. Cdd – 2 sts dec'd; 1 st. Cut yarn and fasten off.

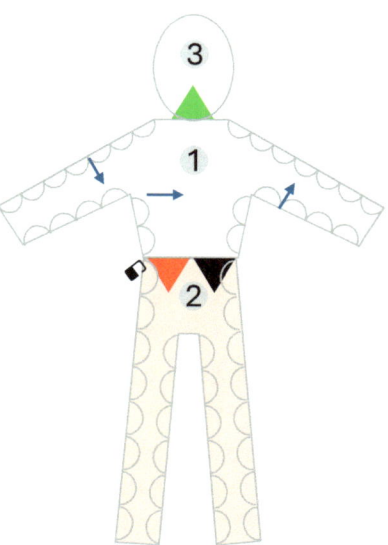

Figure 39: Person construction

TOC

Birds

Thread yarn for Bird onto a tapestry or finishing needle. Insert the needle from back to front of work at the starting location for right-most tip of the bird's right wing. The bird can be oriented horizontally or at a slight angle from horizontal.

Using chain stitch (see instructions on page 35), work 14 chains in the shape of a bird shown in Figure 40, and making stitches about 1 knitted stitch or ridge apart. Insert needle between strands or through a strand.

A photo of the birds worked on Block 5.1 of the sample blanket is provided for additional detail.

On the sample, Birds were added to two Blocks that had large Sky pieces. One bird is between Blocks 2.6 and 2.7, and two birds are on Block 5.1. See the photo of the full blanket on the first page of this pattern for positioning of all embellishments.

Embroidered Birds on Block 5.1. *Note.* The left wing of the lower bird is a bit short because otherwise it would overlap the Border. The shorter wing makes it look like this bird is flying in a different direction from the other bird, which adds interest.

Figure 40: Bird Construction

TOC

JOINING BLOCKS, STRIPS, AND WORKING BORDERS

SEW BLOCKS INTO STRIPS

See Figure 2 on page 5 for layout of Strips. With long tails and mattress st, sew Blocks together. Before starting, watch video at YouTube/@knitwitme.

JOINING STRIPS - see Figure 41

Two adjacent/consecutively numbered Strips are joined pair-wise. The Upper Strip is the lower numbered Strip. Join Strips 1 & 2, 2 & 3, 3 & 4, and 4 & 5 as follows:

PREP UPPER STRIP

With a circular needle, starting at the bottom-left corner of the Upper Strip at green triangle, with SC for Lower Strip, pu&k 260 sts on bottom edge of the strip to corner.

Row 2 (WS): Knit 1 row. Cut yarn. Leave 260 sts on the circular needle and set this piece aside.

PREP LOWER STRIP

With a second circular needle, starting at top-right corner of the Lower Strip at red triangle, with SC for Lower Strip, pu&k 260 sts along top edge of the Strip to corner.

Rows 2 (WS)-4: Knit (2 ridges). Do not cut yarn. Leave 260 sts on the 2nd circular needle.

JOIN WITH 3-NEEDLE BO

Lay the Lower Strip, RS up, on a flat surface with circular needle at top. With its RS facing down, lay Upper Strip on top of Lower Strip, so RS's of Strips face each other and the circular needles are parallel. With working yarn still attached to Lower Strip, 3-needle BO all sts on needles, loosely. Cut yarn, insert end through last loop & tighten.

Note: Use the m's placed every 13th st for alignment. If off by a st, k2tog during the 3-needle BO to eliminate the extra st instead of undoing your BO to retrieve sts. Rm's m's when encountered.

SKY EXTENSION

Starting at the top-right corner of the Blanket, with color for Strip 1's Sky, with circular needle, pu&k 260 sts on the top edge of the blanket. Knit 3 rows/2 ridges. Cut yarn. Leave sts on needle for Top Border.

BORDERS

Do not cut yarn until after Right Border.

TOP BORDER

On RS, with 260 sts still on needle from prev step, with A, knit 12 rows. BO loosely, leaving last st on needle.

LEFT BORDER

Pu&k 6 sts on left edge of Top Border, 344 sts on left edge of blanket (2 sts on Sky Extension, 66 sts per Strip, 3 sts per Join) – 352 sts.

Knit 11 rows. BO loosely, leaving last st on needle.

BOTTOM BORDER

Pu&k 6 sts on bottom edge of Left Border, 260 sts on bottom edge of blanket – 267 sts.

Knit 11 rows. BO loosely, leaving last st on needle.

RIGHT BORDER

Pu&k 6 sts on the right edge of the Bottom Border, 344 sts (66 sts per Strip, and 3 sts per each Join, and 2 sts on Strip Extension) on the right edge, and 7 sts on the right edge of the Top Border - 358 sts.

Knit 11 rows. BO loosely. Cut yarn and fasten off.

TOC

Upper Strip

1

260

2

260

Lower Strip

Figure 41: Joining Strips

Hints

Generate 13, 26 or 39 sts on the edge of a Block, matching the Block's width.

- When live sts on holders are encountered, knit those sts instead of performing pu&k.
- Pm on needle between Blocks so sts don't need to be recounted.
- After all 260 sts are generated, place additional m's so there is a m bet each set of 13 sts. These additional m's help with alignment during Joins.

ABBREVIATIONS
GLOSSARY
PHOTO TUTORIALS
OTHER MATERIALS

ABBREVIATIONS

Bef	Before		**P2sso**	Pass 2 slipped stitches over
Beg	Begin(ning)		**P2tog**	Purl 2 together (1 st dec'd)
Bet	Between		**Patt**	Pattern stitch
Bli	Backwards loop increase		**Pm**	Place marker
BO	Bind off		**Prev**	Previous
Cdd	Central double decrease: Slip 2 sts as if to k2tog, k1, pass slipped sts over (2 sts dec'd)		**Psso**	Pass 1 slipped stitch over
			Pu&k	Pick up & knit
			Pwise	Purlwise
Cdd2	Slip 3 sts as if to k3tog, k2tog, pass slipped sts over (4 sts dec'd)		**R**	Right hand
			Rem	Remain(ing)
Cddp	Slip 2 sts tog, p1, then pass slipped sts over		**Rep(s)**	Repeat(s) (ing)
			Rm	Remove marker
CO	Cast on		**Rnd(s)**	Round(s)
Cont	Continu(e)(ing)		**RS**	Right side
Dec('d)(ing)	Decrease(d)(ing)		**Sk2po**	Slip 1 st knitwise, knit 2 sts together; pass slipped stitch over (2 sts dec'd)
Dpns	Double-pointed needles			
Inc('d)(ing)	Increase(d)(ing)		**Sl**	Slip
K	Knit		**Sm**	Slip marker
K2tog	Knit 2 sts together (1 st dec'd)		**Ssk**	Slip 2 sts knitwise, knit these 2 sts together through back loops (1 st dec'd)
K2togBO	Knit 2 sts together then bind off the resulting stitch (2 sts dec'd)			
Kf&b	Knit into the front leg of the next st, leaving it on the Left needle, then knit into the back leg of the same st, then transfer the st to the Right needle (1 st inc'd)		**Sssk**	Slip 3 sts knitwise and together to the right needle, knit the next 2 sts together, insert left needle, left-to-right, through all 3 slipped sts, and pass over the k2tog st.
			St(s)	Stitch(es)
Koh	Knit off holder		**Tbl**	Through back loop(s)
Kwise	Knitwise		**Tog**	Together
Kyok	(k1, yo, k1) into 1 st (2 sts inc'd)		**W&T**	Wrap & turn
L	Left, left hand		**WS**	Wrong side
M	Marker		**WYIF**	With yarn in front
P	Purl		**Ybck**	Move yarn to the back
			YO	Yarn over

GLOSSARY

Common knitting techniques are on this page, and less common techniques are covered in more depth on the pages that follow.

Techniques with a camera icon have an instructional video. <DT>

Backwards Loop Increase (bli) 📹

*With yarn in back, wrap yarn around left index finger, back to front, once with yarn exiting to right. Insert R needle, right to left, under the front leg of the loop and slip loop off finger and onto R needle. Tighten yarn (1 st inc'd).

Cable BO

K1, bring yarn to front, sl st to L needle, p2tog, *yarn to back, sl 1 st kwise to R needle, sl both sts to L needle, p2tog, yarn to front, sl1 pwise to R needle, sl both sts to L needle, P2tog; rep from *.

I-cord

Set up: Onto a dpn of same size used to work blanket, using provisional technique, CO 3 sts. Starting at the edge location specified in the pattern, *Insert the working needle front to back through next a selvage st, yarn around working needle and pull a loop through. Using the non-working dpn, pass 3rd (last) st on needle over new st],

Slide sts to the other tip of the working needle, k2, insert working needle through next selvage st and knit the 3rd st on the needle and the selvage st together. Rep bet * and * around the blanket, making 2 extra repeats in each corner by inserting the working needle into the same corner stitch 3 times. Graft ends together.

Knitted Cast-on

6 inches from end of yarn, make a slipknot and slide loop onto L needle. *Insert R needle left-to-right through front leg of last-made loop (i.e., kwise), wind working end of yarn around R needle counter-clockwise and pull new loop through existing loop. Transfer new loop on R needle to the L needle. Pull yarn to adjust tension. Rep from * to add more sts. For a tighter BO, insert needle through both legs of the last-made loop.

Pinhole Cast-on

To begin, wrap yarn around index finger twice, making a circle from front to back with working yarn hanging to front.

1. Using a crochet hook, insert hook into circle, bet yarn circle and finger.

2. Draw working yarn through center of circle then draw another loop through the loop on the needle, as for crochet chain st. One st is now complete.

Rep steps [1 & 2] to add additional sts to the crochet hook. Circle may be slipped off finger and held once a few sts have been created. When desired number of sts have been created, transfer sts one-by-one to dpns as instructed by patt. After several rounds are completed, pull tail to tighten center sts and fasten off securely.

Provisional Cast-on

Method 1: Traditional Crochet Chain: Using a crochet hook and contrasting yarn of the same weight as working yarn, make a chain with twice the number of sts as need to be CO plus 1. Using crochet hook and working yarn, insert hook into the back "bump" of the 2nd chain st, draw yarn through and transfer to needle. Rep in every 2nd back bump until the number of sts needed for the CO are on the needle. Begin knitting from these sts.

When provisionally CO sts need to become "live," undo the crochet chain from the end, one stitch at a time, and transfer sts to needle as they become free.

Method 2: Wrapping a Yarn: Use a piece of scrap yarn about 3 times the length of the edge to be cast on. With working yarn, make a slipknot on one end of the scrap yarn, then lay scrap yarn parallel to the needle used for casting on, with the slip knotted end furthest from the needle tip. Wind the working yarn around both the needle and the scrap yarn snugly until there are the same number of winds on needle as needed for the cast-on. Tie ends of the scrap yarn tog. With working yarn, begin work. *Note:* It may be easier to use the cable of an interchangeable needle set or a stitch holder in place of the scrap yarn.

Single Crochet for Edging

*Insert hook through next edge st. Yarn over the hook and draw a yarn loop through the edge stitch. Yarn over the hook again and draw through rem loop(s) on hook. Rep from *.

Slip Stitch (Crochet) for Edging

Insert hook through next edge st. Bring yarn over hook from back to front. Draw the yarn through to the front, then through existing loop on the hook. Repeat.

Tacking Embellishments

When fastening off, leave a long tail. Pin the embellishment to the RS of the work as instructed, inserting pin on the WS so that sewing yarn doesn't get tangled around the pin. Starting at the location where the tail begins, *take a stitch in the front bump of the blanket, just under the edge of the embellishment. To locate this bump, lift the edge of the embellishment slightly to peak underneath. Then take a stitch in the edge (outermost leg) of the embellishment. Rep from * around the entire embellishment, to the starting point. Tie off, then insert the needle back and forth between the embellishment and blanket until the yarn end is ½"/1 cm long, to bury the yarn underneath the embellishment. Carefully trim yarn end flush with the edge of the embellishment.

3-NEEDLE BIND-OFF 📹

The 3-needle bind-off is used to join 2 sets of live stitches and is a great modular method for making a geometric shape.

HOW TO

A 3-needle BO used for joining and shaping is generally commenced after working part or all of a right side row, as follows:

1) On the next (a WS) row, knit half the stitches on the row only.

2) Rotate needles so that tips are parallel, RS are tog, WS facing out. Pull working yarn out from bet needles. The needle closer to you is the front needle, and the one behind is the back needle.

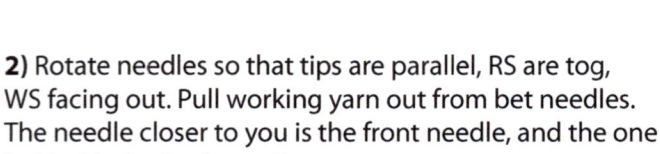

3) Insert third needle, as if to knit, through 1st st on front needle, then 1st st on back needle. Wrap yarn around third needle, as if to knit.

4) With third needle, draw yarn loop through the 1st loop on the back needle, then through 1st loop on the front needle.

5) Slip both stitches off the two needles. There is now one loop on the third needle.

6) Repeat Steps 3 through 5 with the next pair of stitches on the front and back needles.

7) There are now 2 sts on the third needle. Insert the back needle into 2nd (right-most) st on third needle, and pull over the 1st stitch on the third needle, to bind off.

8) Now there is just 1 stitch remaining on the third needle. Repeat Steps 6 and 7 until there are no stitches remaining on the front and back needles and 1 st remaining on the third needle. Follow pattern instructions for handling the remaining stitch.

HINTS FOR SUCCESS

- Avoid dropping stitches by keeping the front and back needle tips aligned, working near the needle tips, and using your left index finger to prevent stitches on the back needle from falling off.

- If there are too many stitches on the front needle, decrease during the BO by inserting the third needle through 2 stitches on the front needle, instead of just 1 st. Likewise, if there are too many stitches on the back needle, insert the third needle through 2 sts on the back needle. Space out multiple decreases evenly over the BO.

- A BO that is too tight will distort the shape. If your BO tends to be tight, choose a larger size needle as your third needle.

BORDERS AND BACKINGS

BORDERS

Each blanket in this book has a border selected to complement the blanket. This section has ideas and how-to instructions for alternate border treatments.

A border provides a consistent and flat edging that doesn't curl or distort. It terminates the pattern by framing the design elements. Audition different colors for the border to see what the blanket needs to look complete. Using a dominant color from the blanket makes the border part of the design. A more muted version of a color in the blanket or a neutral color will frame the blanket without drawing attention or competing with the design.

LOG CABIN see Figure 42

A Log Cabin border is used when the Border is worked in a single color. It is used in most of the blankets in this book. "Nr," is the number of complete ridges knitted in the Border. The number of stitches to pu&k on the short edge of a completed border is 1 + Nr.

JOIN-AS-YOU-GO BORDER (JAYG)

Figure 42: Construction of a Log Cabin Border

If you don't have a circular needle, a JAYG border can be worked counterclockwise around the blanket starting at the middle of an edge, using two dpns. CO 5 to 10 stitches (aka Border stitches). Knit all rows, making a join to the blanket edge at the end of every RS row by inserting the R needle through the back loop of the last Border stitch, and the edge of the blanket. Use the original instructions from the blanket's Border for the number of Joins to make per shape along the blanket's edge.

At corners, use the following pattern stitch to turn the corner. <DT>39

Row 1 (RS): Knit to last st, wrap & turn (w&t) last st.

Row 2 (WS): Knit.

Row 3: Knit to 1 st before prev wrap, w&t next stitch.

Row 4: Knit.

Rep [Rows 3 and 4] until the 2nd st from the beginning of the RS row is wrapped.

Next RS row: K1, w&t.

Note: In this phase, we are wrapping stitches for the second time.

Next WS row: Knit.

Row 5: Knit to end including the stitch that was wrapped on the prev RS row, w&t next stitch.

Row 6: Knit.

Repeat [Rows 5 & 6] until the last st on a RS row is wrapped.

Next WS Row: Knit.

CROCHET BORDER

A scalloped crocheted edge is fast and attractive. With yarn and crochet hook, on RS, attach yarn to center of right edge of blanket face by pulling loop up from back of work. Ch1. *Skip 2 garter st ridges/CO/BO sts and make 7 double crochet (dc) in next ridge/st, skip 2 garter st ridges/CO/BO sts and make sl st in next ridge/CO/BO st.*

Rep between * and *, to end of edge making adjustments if needed to end the scallop exactly at the corner. Sl st in the blanket corner, ch3, sl st in same corner location, and continue scallops on the next border. When the starting point is reached, sl st in the initial chain stitch. Cut yarn, fasten off and weave in ends. If there are diagonal pieces on the blanket edge, you may first work a single crochet around the entire blanket, making 1 sc for each st that would have otherwise been pu&k on the pieces.

BACKING A BLANKET

A fabric backing adds a nice finish to a knitted blanket, makes it warmer, reduces stretch, and allows you to skip the weaving in.

Select a fabric for the backing. For the lightest backing, use double gauze. A good option for a non-stretch backing is double-brushed flannel. It is warm, strong, affordable, and easy to work with. Double-brushed flannels are fuzzy on both sides, which helps the fabric stick to the knitted blanket, requiring less tacking in the middle of the blanket. Fleece, a synthetic, is thicker and stretchier than flannel. If the blanket is wool, or extra warmth is desired, use a woven wool fabric for the backing.

Prepare the blanket by blocking it, following the laundering instructions on the yarn label.

Mark the center of the blanket with a stitch marker by folding it into quarters with right sides together and corners aligned.

On a large surface, spread out and flatten the blanket, right side down, so it lays flat and is not skewed. Using masking or painter's tape edges to the work surface so they don't move.

Measure the width of the blanket in several places, average, and record. Do the same for the length.

Determine the fabric requirements. If the width of the fabric, after selvages are removed, is smaller than the width of the blanket, the amount of fabric needed will be 2 times the blanket length.

If the width of the fabric is the same or more than the width of the blanket then the amount of fabric needed is the same as the length of the blanket.

Prepare the fabric. Cotton fabric should be washed, dried, and pressed to remove wrinkles, following manufacturer's instructions. Before washing the fabric, cut off all the selvage edges (where the printing is) because they shrink at a faster rate than the fabric.

Construct the fabric backing. The backing will be the same size as the blanket.

Measure the fabric. If the blanket is wider than the fabric, sew two widths of fabric together to span the width. It will be easiest with a sewing machine but can be done by hand. With RS of the fabric together, sew a vertical seam, leaving a ½"/1.25 cm seam allowance. Press the seam out flat. When seaming together two lengths of fabric, it is more aesthetically pleasing to cut one in half along the vertical, and center the uncut piece between the two halves. For design interest, piece together a backing from smaller pieces of fabric. Using a bed sheet avoids seaming, but the high thread count of most sheets makes sewing by hand tiring.

Mark the center of the backing by folding it in half twice, matching corners exactly, then inserting a safety pin through the corner of the folds.

Center the fabric, right side up, on top of the blanket using this approach:

> With the backing folded in quarters with right sides together, place it on the blanket, matching the marked center of the backing with the marked

center of the blanket, then unfold the backing carefully, maintaining alignment of the centers of the fabric and blanket.

Trim the backing almost even with the blanket edge, cutting ⅛"/.3 cm to ¼"/.6 cm outside the blanket edge. Be careful not to cut the blanket.

Proceed in one of the following ways:

1) With safety pins, lift the backing edge slightly and turn in a ½"/1.25 cm hem and finger press, then insert a safety pin through the turned hem and the knitted blanket edge to secure. Continue around the blanket in this manner to pin the edge in place.

2) Separate the layers and with a hot iron, press a ½"/1.25 cm hem all around the edge of the backing. *Optional*: Using a 3 mm long straight stitch, sew the hem down ¼"/.6 cm from the edge around entire perimeter of the fabric piece. Reassemble and align the center of the backing and blanket, wrong sides together, as they were initially, and use safety pins to pin them together.

Sewing the layers must be done by hand. With the fabric side facing up, a sewing needle and sewing thread that matches the border color, and using whip stitch, sew the hem of the fabric to the back of the border making a stitch about every ¼"/.6 cm. The fabric hem will lie about ½"/1.25 cm in from the blanket edge. So that thread doesn't show on the knitted blanket side, take stitches into the bumps of the garter stitch ridges whenever possible.

Lay the blanket out flat again with the knitted side up. Take a few discrete stitches through both layers in about 8–10 different locations scattered around the blanket surface. Hide the thread ends between layers. This should be enough to keep the layers together during use and laundering.

TOC

INTARSIA ◯◀

Intarsia is used when a large one-color motif is to be added. For example, the large pink heart in the left of Figure 43 should be worked in intarsia. If you imagine knitting across a row in the heart area of the top, you first knit with the background (peach) color then the pink heart color, and finally with the background color. That row slice only has 3 colors.

Rule for Intarsia: When the row has a small number of colors compared to the number of stitches on the needle, and there are large numbers of contiguous stitches worked in each color of yarn, use intarsia.

Contrast that top with one in the center of Figure 43. Imagine you are knitting across one of the rows in the heart section and are alternating frequently between the background and heart colors.

Rule for Stranded: When switching between the background color and contrast color often and predictably (in a repeating pattern), use stranded (aka "fair isle").

What about the design on the far-right of Figure 43 with the hearts staggered diagonally? This is a murky situation. It doesn't meet the requirements for stranded because the heart pattern doesn't repeat across the row, but the hearts are very small so it doesn't meet the requirement for intarsia where the area of contrast color is large. For this area you could either work it in intarsia or in duplicate stitch or a combination of the two.

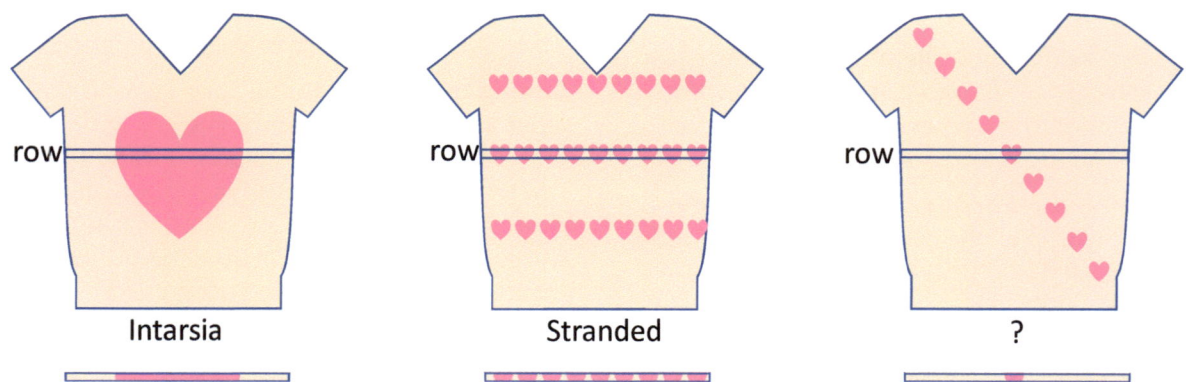

Figure 43: Selecting the Right Technique for Colorwork

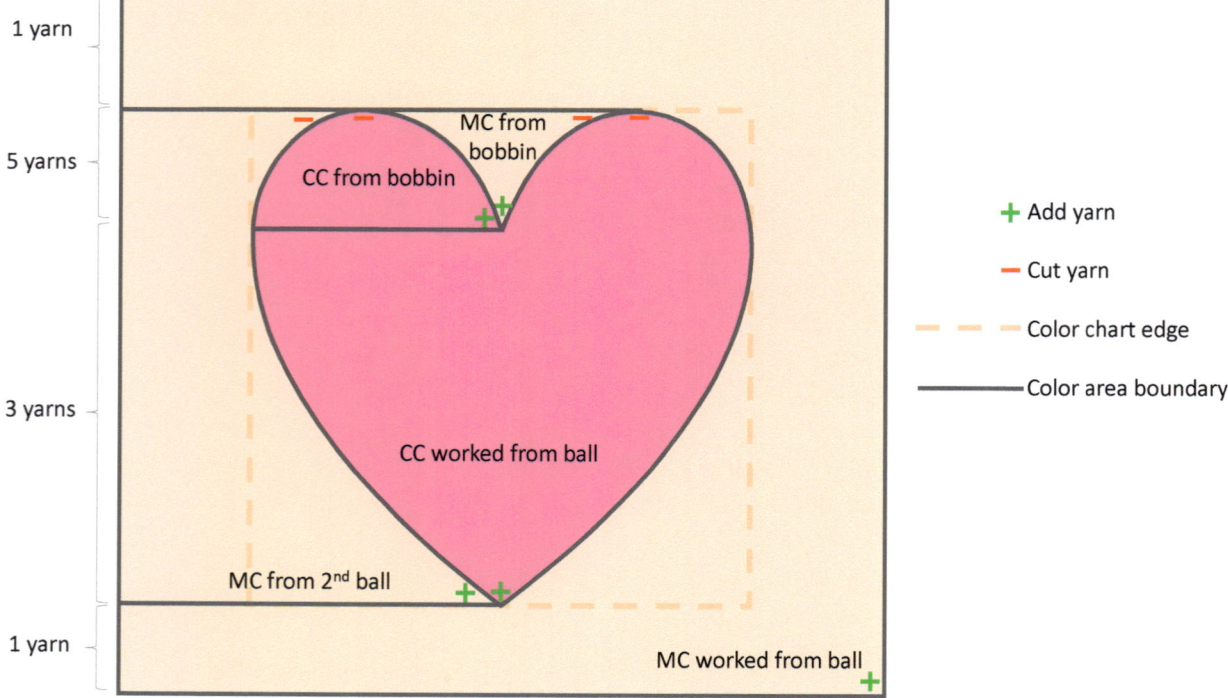

Figure 44: Adding and Cutting Yarn

How It works

With intarsia, a separate yarn strand (ball) is needed for each noncontiguous area of color, as shown in Figure 46. In most of this Heart design there are 3 balls of yarn active at a time, but when we get to the row where the lobes split, 5 balls are needed until the heart is complete. Once the heart is complete, all four "extra" yarns that were added are cut, and the work continues with the main ball.

When knitting a row, each yarn is positioned at the right edge of the area to be worked in that color. When working across the row the yarn is dropped at the left edge of the color area, and the new color is picked up. Figure 46 shows the positions of the yarn balls at the beginning and end of a row. When the work is turned for starting the next row, the yarn ball positions are automatically at the right edge of each color area, just where they need to be to work the next row.

Intarsia designs are described via a color chart. The chart in Figure 45 contains 50 rows and is 25 stitches wide. For each row the chart specifies the stitch to use and the color to work the stitch. For instance, on Row 1, work sts 1–12 in MC, stitch 13 in CC, and stitches 14–25 in MC.

This chart is for garter stitch so it looks different than color charts you may have worked for stockinette stitch. A garter stitch chart will look elongated (stretched) when compared with the final knitted piece. On a chart, each stitch is represented by a square, but in garter stitch each ridge is 1 st wide and 2 sts tall. Every row is knitted so on WS rows there is a dot symbol indicating to knit on the WS. In some patterns, simple edge shaping is combined with intarsia, so there will be k2tog or ssk symbols on some rows. Some of the intarsia charts in this book only include RS rows. It is assumed the WS rows are knitted in the same color as the prev RS row.

In some patterns, there will be estimated yarn amounts for areas that should be worked from bobbins. Use those amounts as estimates then adjust yardage to actual use after the chart is worked the first time. Another way to

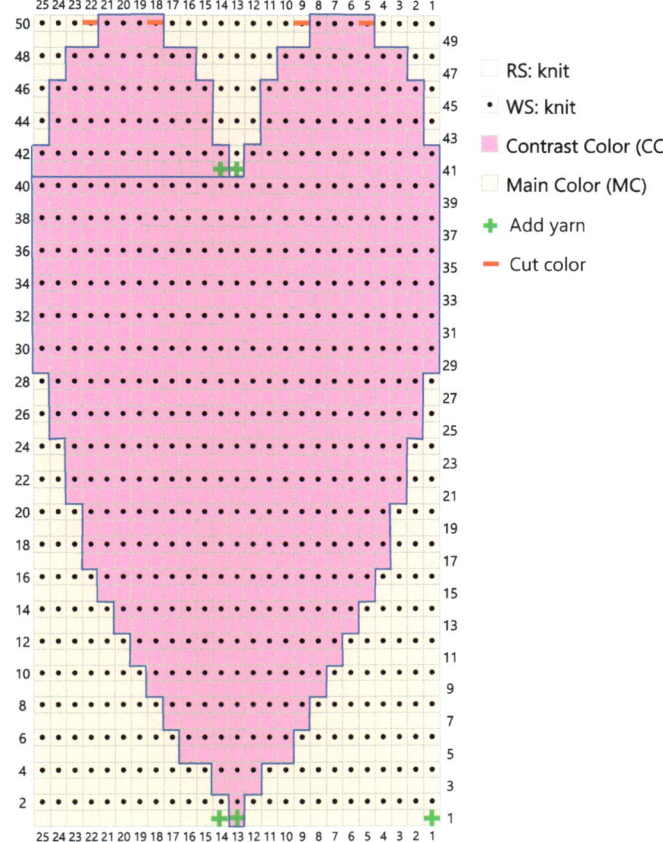

RS: knit

• **WS: knit**

▨ **Contrast Color (CC)**

☐ **Main Color (MC)**

✚ **Add yarn**

━ **Cut color**

Figure 45: Heart Chart

At the beginning of each row, yarns are at right edge of their color sections.

When the row is completed, yarns are now at the left edge of their color section. So, when work is turned, yarns are again at the right edge.

Note: A separate yarn strand (ball) is required for each noncontiguous color section.

Figure 46: Yarn Ball Positions for Intarsia at Beginning and End of Rows

estimate the length of yarn needed is to work an area from the ball, undo those rows, and measure how much yarn was used.

Added to this chart (Figure 45) are some additional symbols and outlines that show when to add and cut yarn. The dark gray lines enclose areas where separate yarns are used. The green plus sign indicates where to add yarn, and the red minus sign is where yarn is cut. A suggestion is made as to whether to work the yarn directly from the ball or to wind yarn onto a bobbin. It is not practical to put very long lengths of yarn onto a bobbin, but smaller areas that require less yardage may be knit from bobbins to help with yarn management.

Yarns are not cut until a color area is complete.

AVOIDING HOLES

When making color changes (dropping Old Yarn and continuing with New Yarn), we need to do something special to connect the yarns, otherwise we will have independent columns of stitches at the color transitions and holes in the knitting.

This *something* is to cross the yarns. How to cross depends on whether we're working a RS or WS row.

RS row yarn changes/crossing (see Figure 47): Yarns are already on the WS of the work because we are knitting. Take the Old Yarn (yarn that is about to be dropped) and cross it over and to the left of the New Yarn on the WS of the work, pick up the New Yarn color, draw up any extra slack yarn, and continue.

> *Old Yarn over New Yarn,*
> *continue with New Yarn.*

WS row yarn changes/crossing (see Figure 48): A WS row is always knitted, which means that the Old Yarn (yarn that is about to be dropped) is away from you, on the RS of the work. Yarn crossing must always occur with both the yarns on the WS of the work, so move the Old Yarn (the yarn that is about to be dropped) between the needles and toward you (to the WS) and move it to the left so that it crosses over the New Yarn. Move the New Yarn between the needles to the RS of the work (away from you), draw up extra yarn and continue knitting with the New Yarn.

> *Old Yarn forward, Old Yarn left over New Yarn, New Yarn to back,*
> *continue with New Yarn.*

Despite crossing yarns there will still be small holes next to locations where yarn was added and cut. Thread the yarn end onto a tapestry needle and on the WS, insert needle through the bump of the stitch of different color next to the hole, then back through the first stitch. On the WS, weave in yarn.

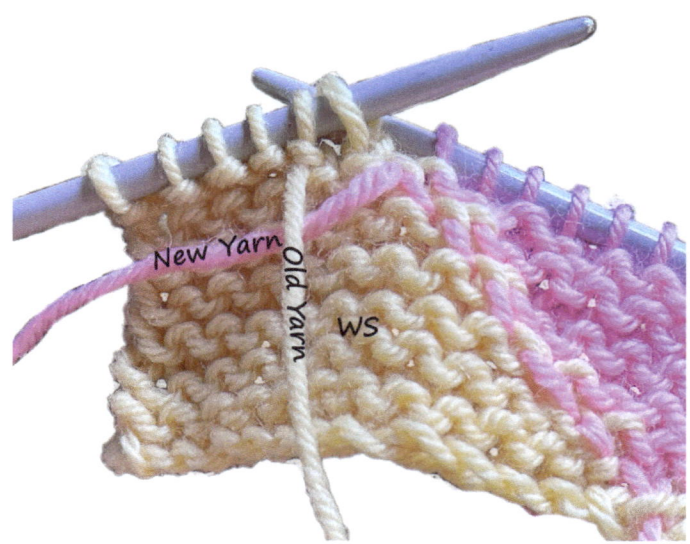

Figure 47: RS Row: Yarn "cross" while working a RS show, but shown on the WS, is shown above. Crossing yarns is always done on the WS. New Yarn goes under Old Yarn.

Figure 48: WS Row: Initially, the Old Yarn is away from you on RS as shown here. Now bring Old Yarn forward (to WS) and then to the left, holding it in place with the left thumb. Then move the New Yarn away from you (between the needle and to the RS) and continue knitting with New Yarn.

TOC

MATTRESS STITCH

Sewing garter stitch pieces together with mattress stitch produces the neatest and most invisible seam.

WHEN TO USE MATTRESS STITCH

Mattress stitch can be used to sew together: Side edge to side edge, CO edge to CO edge, CO edge to BO edge, or side edge to CO/BO edge. We focus on side edge to side edge, which is the most common.

HOW TO SEAM WITH MATTRESS STITCH

1) Thread long CO/BO tail or yarn the color of one of the pieces onto tapestry needle.

Insert up through the first edge bump of the piece opposite where the yarn is emerging. In this example the yarn is emerging from the left piece so we insert first through the right edge, then through the first edge bump of the left edge.

Pull yarn to eliminate some but not all of the slack.

2) Insert needle upwards through the next bump on the right edge, and pull to eliminate slack.

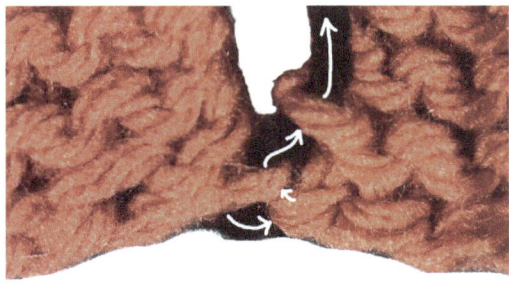

3) Continue inserting tapestry needle upwards through alternating left and right edge bumps.

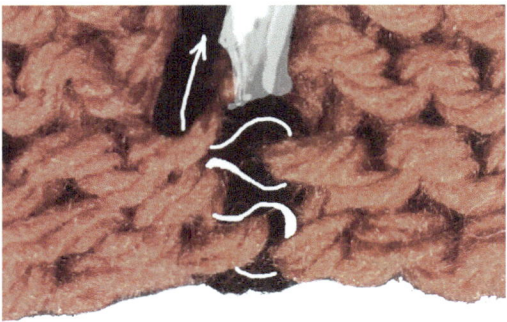

ALIGNING COLOR STRIPES

Aligning color transitions presents a challenge because the ridges of one edge will nest in the valleys of the other edge, causing striping to appear slightly misaligned (aka "jogging") along the seam. To align stripes, we will need to do an "around the world" maneuver as shown below.

1) Insert needle upwards through the last edge bump of the old color on the left edge.

On the right edge, insert needle downwards through the last edge bump of the old color.

2) Insert needle upwards through the last bump on the left edge, again. Draw up slack.

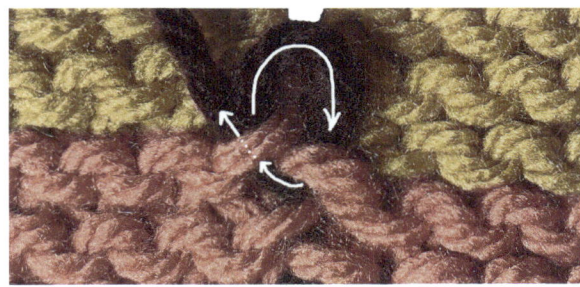

3) Unthread and trim current sewing yarn. Thread new yarn color onto needle, and continue.

Note: Sts before the "around the world" are blue, "around the world" sts are white, and sts in the new yarn color are pink.

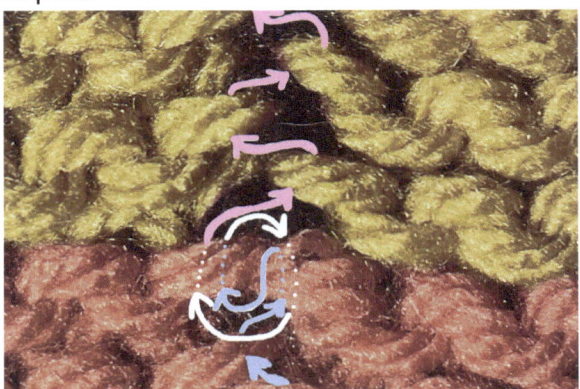

PICK UP AND KNIT (PU&K) 📹

Pick Up & Knit (pu&k) is a technique used to generate live stitches on the edge of a previously completed piece (PCP) of knitting. It is used in modular knitting in place of sewing pieces together.

Pu&k differs from *picking up* stitches because a loop of working yarn is drawn through a small hole made by poking a knitting needle or crochet hook through the edge of the PCP. With *picking up,* the needle is loaded with loops of yarn that are *picked up* or *borrowed* from the PCP's edge.

When pu&k'ing on an edge perpendicular to (at right angles to) a CO/BO edge, as shown in Figure 51, 1 st is generated per every two rows of knitting. Two rows of knitting form an easily recognized surface feature on the knitting called a "ridge" as shown in Figure 50. The area between ridges is referred to as the "valley."

Start pu&k at location indicated in pattern. Hold the working yarn in your left hand and provide the proper tension by winding the yarn over and under your fingers.

For the neatest result, insert through bumps when available. A bump is the last st of a ridge. Working on the RS, and with a knitting needle, insert front to back through the next bump and draw a yarn loop to front of work. If working on the left or right edge that has no shaping, insert needle through each bump on the edge. If more sts are needed than there are bumps available, insert into the outside strand of the edge stitch bet ridges (aka, the "valley"). If working on a CO or BO edge, insert the needle through both strands of yarn.

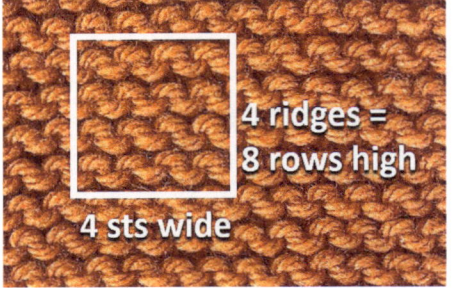

Figure 50: 4 Ridges High by 4 Stitches Wide

Bind-off Edge

Perpendicular (w.r.t. BO/CO) Edge

Cast-on Edge

Figure 51: Identification of Edges

When picking up on a 45 degree diagonal edge, as shown in Figure 49, *pu&k in two consecutive ridges, then in the valley bef the next ridge; rep from * cont this cadence. When close to the ending point, count the sts generated and plan out the remaining pu&k locations. If the stitch count is incorrect by a few sts, make increases (bli) or decreases (k2tog) on the next WS row. Place markers as a reminder, where a marker through 2 sts indicates a planned decrease (k2tog) and a marker through 1 st indicates a planned increase (bli).

A crochet hook may be used instead of a knitting needle. If using a crochet hook, use the same size (in mm) as the working knitting needle or up to 0.5 mm smaller than needle size. If working with a crochet hook, sts may be accumulated on the crochet hook's shaft, then transferred off the non-hook end to needle. The crochet hook must have a thin shank.

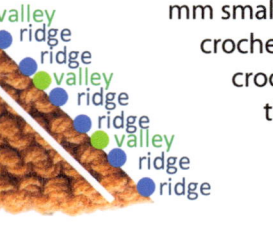

ridge
valley

45 degrees w.r.t. co/bo

valley
ridge
ridge
valley
ridge
ridge
valley
ridge
ridge

Figure 49: Pu&k on Diagonal Edge

TOC

SLIP STITCH TRAVELING

Slip stitch traveling is used to move the working yarn to a new location along an edge that will later be sewn to another piece. The purpose is to avoid cutting yarn, which generates more ends to weave in, and to produce a neat and regular edge to which other pieces may be sewn. The pattern's instructions will state how many stitches to work along an edge.

How to

1) In this example we want to move the working yarn from point A to B.

3) Insert L needle, left to right, through the front leg of the right-most stitch on the R needle and slip stitch over the left-most stitch. 1 stitch remains on the R needle. Adjust tension so that edge does not pull in.

2) Using a crochet hook or knitting needle (latter shown here) and working on the RS, insert R needle front to back through the outer leg of the edge stitch of the first valley, yarn around counter-clockwise, and pull a loop through. There are now 2 stitches on the needle.

4) Repeat Steps 2 and 3 along the edge to B, inserting R needle into the next valley.

Note: If ridges are perpendicular to edge, insert in every valley. If ridges are diagonal to edge, insert needle in every valley and in every other ridge in order to generate enough stitches. Stop occasionally to count stitches and plan out the remainder of the locations for inserting needle.

The slipped stitches should look like chaining.

Ridges Diagonal to edge – insert needle into every valley and every other ridge

Ridges Perpendicular to edge – insert needle in every valley

TOC

TACKING DRAPED YARN 📹

When an edge of knitting will later have stitches picked up and knitted (pu&k) along it, pattern instructions may say to drape yarn between uses instead of cutting and reattaching. Later, during a pu&k on the same edge, the draped yarn will be tacked to the edge. This reduces the number of yarn ends to weave in during finishing and saves yarn.

HOW TO

1) When draping, leave about ½"/1.25 cm extra for every 1"/2.5 cm that yarn must be carried. Another way to get the right amount of drape is to stretch the edge of the garter stitch, and leave enough draped yarn to span the stretched edge.

3) And on the next stitch, shown here, the needle is inserted OVER the draped yarn.

2) Later, when performing pu&k along an edge with a draped yarn, alternate inserting the R needle over and under the draped yarn. In the photo below, the needle is being inserted UNDER the draped yarn.

4) The WS of the completed pu&k shows that the mint green draped yarn is now neatly tacked to the edge of the orange stripe.

TOC

WRAP & TURN (W&T) 🎥

Wrap & turn, aka short rows, is used to work only some of the stitches in a row. In apparel knitting it is used for shoulder shaping, sock heels, and bust darts. In geometric knitting it is used to create curved shapes.

HOW TO WRAP & TURN

When instructed to wrap & turn you will be wrapping the next stitch on the L needle, and turning the work, leaving the remaining stitches unworked.

Whether working a RS or WS row, to wrap the next stitch, do as follows:

1. Work to the indicated turning point, slip the next stitch purlwise to the R needle.

2. Bring yarn forward.

3. Turn work (the slipped stitch is now on the L needle and the yarn is now at the back of the work), leaving rem sts of row unworked.

4. Insert R needle purlwise into the *slipped stitch* and slip it (again) back to the R needle.

5. Begin working the following row as instructed by the pattern.

TENSIONING THE WRAP

When wrapping the stitch do not leave a lot of loose yarn. Wrap it snugly.

WHAT'S DIFFERENT ABOUT GARTER STITCH?

In w&t for stockinette stitch, the wrap and the wrapped stitch are knitted together on the following row to avoid the little hole that normally forms.

But in garter stitch, we don't do this. On the following row, the wrapped stitch is just knitted. Nothing special needs to be done with the wrap. And there will not be a noticeable hole in the fabric because garter stitch is denser and the surface ridges hide the wraps that are in the *valleys* between ridges.

HOW TO DETERMINE WHICH SIDE IS THE RS

All the turning of the work can cause you to lose track of which side is the RS. In garter stitch knitting, the front and back of the work look the same until color changes begin. Therefore, mark the RS of your work with a locking stitch marker. To determine which is the RS, note the position of the CO tail, which is on the bottom-right corner of the RS. If it is on the bottom-left corner you are looking at the WS. Recall that for the patterns in this book you are always using a knitted CO and the cast on counts as Row 1, (see General Notes on page 39).

PERFECT OPPORTUNITY TO PURL BACKWARDS

Also, so that you don't have to turn your work at all, you can purl backwards on WS rows. In this case you work Steps 1 and 2 of the w&t, with the current side still facing you, slip the slipped stitch back to the L needle then begin purling backwards the stitches on the R needle. *Note*: By purling backwards you are working a WS row with the RS facing you, so if there is a wrap & turn instruction on the RS row, you will do this:

1. Slip the stitch to be wrapped from R to L needle.

2. Move yarn from front to back of work.

3. Slip *slipped stitch* from L to R needle.

4. Begin knitting RS stitches.

Note: German short rows; don't worry if you don't know what that is... Suffice it to say that it does not work well for garter stitch.

Figure 52: The flower petals in Flower Show use wrap & turn. The rows that use wrap & turn are the ones where the yellow ridges do not extend all the way to the magenta center.

TOC

WEAVING IN ENDS

When the wrong, or "private," side of the work will be seen, the best but not the fastest way to weave in ends is to work duplicate stitch on the WS of the work, The advantages are: 1) It is less visible on the WS, 2) it is more secure because the yarn ends are buried and won't poke out later, 3) there is no need to fasten off because the friction of the yarn will keep it securely in place, 4) it saves yarn because only 6"/15 cm of yarn is needed *if* you use a Susan Bates Finishing needle (recommended).

How To

If using a tapestry needle, leave a yarn end of 8"/20 cm, and if using a Susan Bates Finishing Needle, leave 6"/15 cm. Don't fasten off, unless the yarn is very slippery, like silk. Thread the yarn end onto the needle.

On the WS, near the place where the yarn emerges from the work, select a ridge of the same color yarn as the end to be woven in. Observe the smiley and frowny faces of the ridge. Now follow Steps 1–7.

1) Insert needle upwards through nearest smiley face, and pull yarn through.

3) Follow the yarn strand down and insert needle right to left underneath the stitch below the current smiley face and pull yarn through.

2) Following the yarn strand around the frowny face, insert needle downwards through next smiley face and pull yarn through.

4) Repeat Steps 1-3 following the strand until about 1"/2.5 cm of yarn remains (3"/7.5 cm if using tapestry needle).

TOC

5) Working from left to right, insert needle between the stitches being duplicated (orange) and the duplicate stitches (blue) and pull yarn through.

7) Turn work over and observe the slight shadow stitches on the RS. When worked in matching yarn color, these will not show.

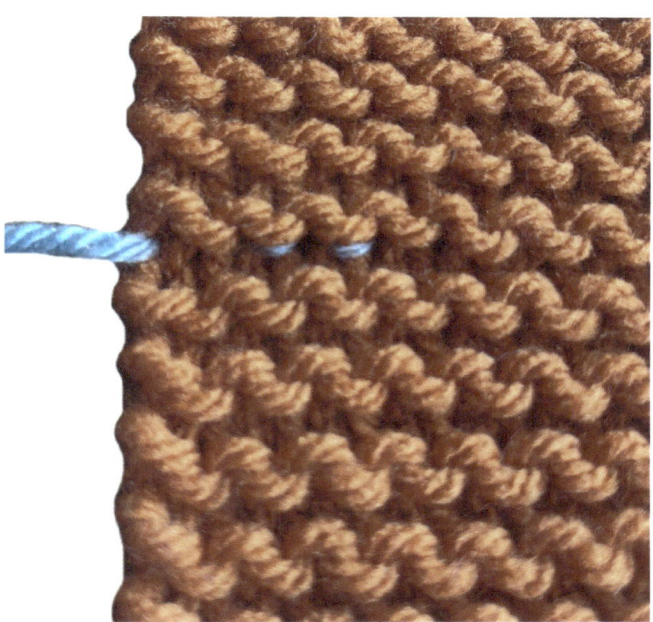

6) Stretch knitting along ridges to see if end will nest. If necessary, trim yarn end flush with edge.

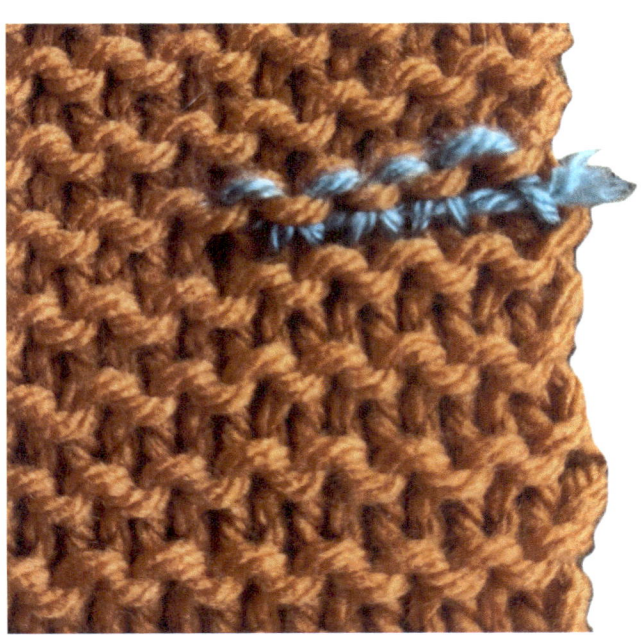

This is the WS of the Flower Show Block with 10 yarn ends woven in with duplicate stitch. *Note.* The interleaved stitches around the magenta center are from pu&k weaving of draped yarn not duplicate stitch weaving. The chaining around the Petals is from pu&k for the Edge and Corner pieces. The duplicate stitches cannot be found, which brings me to my final point: Don't weave in using this method if there is any possibility you need to unravel your piece!

Final Tip: Tension of the duplicate stitches should match the tension of the stitches being duplicated.

TOC

www.ingramcontent.com/pod-product-compliance
Lightning Source LLC
Chambersburg PA
CBHW041553120626
46551CB00002B/187